The Gallery Trilogy: 3 Plays

The Gallery Trilogy: 3 Plays

Casey Ross

The Geeky Press
Indianapolis, IN

Contents

About The Gallery Trilogy

The Gallery Trilogy: Three Plays by Casey Ross includes the full series of Ross's three plays that follow 10 years of a friendship between two disparate artist-best friends. Conceived when Ross was in school at alma mater, Hanover College, the goal of these three plays was to follow and age a set of characters through the actual amount of years between play premieres. The writer was to grow up with the characters. All three of these plays were originally produced through the IndyFringe Festival as episodic chapters and have become local favorites. Art acts as a metaphor for life in these modern sharp-witted plays, as we follow Jackson's unswayable passion and Frank's perhaps self-stifling technique over 10 remarkably human years.

"If Gallery were a book, I'd eagerly be awaiting the sequel." –Hope Baugh, Indy Theatre Habit

"A funny love story, but without the sex. It's more important than that." –John Belden, The Midwest Eagle

"A highlight of the IndyFringe." –Joe Boling, IndianaAuditions.com

Foreword to The Gallery Trilogy: 3 Plays by Casey Ross

If you've gotten to the point of reading the Foreword to this trilogy of three connected plays by the talented and prolific Casey Ross, you probably already know something of her work if you are an Indianapolis theatre-goer. She and *Catalyst Repertory Theatre*, the company she founded in 2014, are rising stars of the Indianapolis theatre scene.

Or perhaps you are looking for plays that are relatively easy to produce and that speak with dramatic perception of and to Millennials with themes of urban life-style, connection, creative expression, and the difficult path to fulfillment

In either case you are looking at the right book!

I've known Casey since I was one of her theatre profs at Hanover College. All educational theatre departments go through up-and-down cycles; Ross' class of '08 was most assuredly an "up" one at Hanover in the creative ambitions and accomplishments of its members. Casey was one of its leaders from her freshmen year on, and that propensity for leadership has led directly to the writing of these three plays.

Beginning as an actress as most young theatre students do, Casey's gift for playwriting became apparent in her junior-year playwriting class. Immediately post her senior year, we produced in our mainstage season her first full-length play, *Slaying the Dragon*, a delightful comedy-fantasy and our entry that year in the American College Theatre Festival. Very near the same time, she premiered off-campus the first play in this trilogy, *Gallery*, in the previous year's IndyFringe Festival.

After graduation her momentum only increased. She was soon writing scripts for the Shawnee Summer Theatre's Children's Theatre Workshops, and the appeal of her plays helped to grow the program to nearly double its size.

I like to think that her real "trench" training in the theatre craft came with her season with the Missoula Children's Theatre, where she a member of a small company of touring artists who, in the span of a one-week community residency in small towns throughout Montana and the rest of the country, created an original musical show with however many young people signed up to be in it. Dare one say, it was the task that Shakespeare faced — creating theatre for the situation and the talent you have, and making it work.

In 2014, Ross's self-proclaimed home-base, the IndyFringe, celebrated its 10th anniversary, leading her to reprise her successful *Gallery* with the sequel play, *Portraits*. She completed the trilogy this year with *Canvas*.

These plays are about the New York art scene and the ten-year story of a 'family' of artsy friends and lovers, looking for connection and meaningful fulfillment in art and each other. There's fiery Jackson Bell, a bad-boy artist who never censors himself, neither in art nor in life, to the detriment of his career and the frustration of those who love him. His best friend is Frank Burnem, an art professor who has struggled with his long-time, more-than-just-friends feelings for the straight Jackson, who also loves Frank but "not in that way". They grew up together with Monica Graham, now a gallery owner and Jackson's ex-wife, who in the first play, *Gallery*, faces her own crisis of "fulfillment" when her struggling art gallery is threatened. Two secondary characters round out this gallery – Frank's brother Martin, and his on-again, off-again lover Scott.

The three plays tell of ten years in their densely interconnected and intertwined lives, dealing with crises that come from the world around them, and too often their own making. Though they can be selfish and self-centered (they are artists, after all!), and too-often blind to their own complicity in the drama of their lives, Ross clearly has great love for these characters and their enduring love for each other. That mutual affection, care, and forgiveness is at the center of the plays.

If you are considering producing these plays, you will not find another playwright-collaborator more theatre-savvy and passionate in her own (good!) way. She will be welcome visitor to your rehearsal room, for she is an accomplished actress as well and realizes that plays are never finished, a playwright finally just moves on, and so she looks always to actors to reveal the truth of the moment. Reading for the first time the brand-new final play of the set, *Canvas*, I find that there are perhaps sequences that Casey will want to tweak here and there, as happens inevitably when new plays go into rehearsal. But these would be minor edits I'm sure; these plays are fully-formed, and provide rich and satisfying material for directors, actors, and audiences.

And if simply reading these plays was your reason for picking up this book, you can look forward to this opportunity to meet Casey Ross through her work, and you'll surely want to attend one of her performances at *Catalyst*. Enjoy the journey.

You go girl!

Paul Hildebrand

April 2017

PART I

Gallery

Gallery is Ross's first play, completed at alma mater, Hanover College, in 2007. It later premiered through the generous support of the Tom Evans Emerging Artist grant at the Indy Fringe Festival later that year, at Theatre on the Square's second stage. The original cast was:

- Jackson Bell played by Nick J. Murray

- Frank Burnem played by Dane Rogers

- Monica Graham played by Erin Cohenour

- Martin Burnem played by Ian McCabe

This play is dedicated to Nick, Dane, Erin, and Ian for being the first breath of life and for forever haunting these people with bits of your indelible qualities. You own every real dent on these human soup cans.

- Jackson Bell: 27, a fiery young artist, passionate, never censors himself.

- Frank Burnem: 30, Jackson's best friend. An art professor, tentative and kind

- Monica Graham: 20s, a savvy art gallery owner, friend of Jackson and Frank

- Martin Burnem: Frank's younger brother, Insensitive and callous.

- Scott: The coffee refill guy. (May be portrayed in café scenes if director desires, as character appears in future one-acts of the series.)

Setting

The settings should be young and modest, suggesting that of a bohemian lifestyle, or that of the cliché "starving artist."

Time

The Present

(In two down spots on either side of stage, stand Frank Burnem and Jackson Bell. They are unaware of each other and address the audience. As they do so, the pace of the scene gradually becomes more urgent.)

FRANK

It's all about technique…

JACKSON

Passion.

FRANK

Following the formulas.

JACKSON

Breaking the rules.

FRANK

Learning how to do it better.

JACKSON

Telling them why they are wrong.

FRANK

Listening…

JACKSON

Paying no attention.

FRANK

Structure.

JACKSON

Concept.

FRANK

The process.

JACKSON

The product.

FRANK

That they like it…

JACKSON

Or, hate it.

FRANK

Art.

JACKSON

Art.

FRANK

My career.

JACKSON

My passion.

FRANK

A living.

JACKSON

A way of life.

FRANK

What I do.

JACKSON

What I must.

FRANK

Educated. Controlled.

JACKSON

Emotional. Rebellious.

FRANK

Speaking to the audience.

JACKSON

Screaming *at* the audience.

FRANK

An exchange.

JACKSON

A monologue.

FRANK

For someone.

JACKSON

For myself.

FRANK

Subtle.

JACKSON

Loud.

FRANK

Modest.

JACKSON

Forward.

FRANK

Fearful…

JACKSON

Fearless.

FRANK

Secretive.

JACKSON

Nothing to hide.

FRANK

What I want to be…

JACKSON

Who I am.

FRANK

What I want to say…

JACKSON

How I can say it.

FRANK

Beautiful deception.

JACKSON

The ugly truth.

FRANK/JACKSON

Art.

(Lights out on both men. When lights return, Monica and Frank stand outside of a high rise business complex. Monica checks her watch while Frank paces around.)

MONICA

Late.

FRANK

He'll be here.

MONICA

No, Frank. Look at us, here *we* are with…our asses and *reputations* on the line…And he's-

FRANK

Doing community service?

MONICA

Late.

FRANK

Something came up.

MONICA

Do you really believe that?

FRANK

No.

MONICA

Then why do you say it?

FRANK

I don't know. More of a formality than a statement of belief I guess…

MONICA

(Checking her watch.)

Five past…

FRANK

So…What did you tell this guy about our boy?

MONICA

(Releasing something between and laugh and a sigh.)

Not that he's punctual…

FRANK

And?

MONICA

I said he's unique.

FRANK

Unique?

MONICA

Well…How would *you* describe him?

FRANK

Not unique.

MONICA

Why not unique?

FRANK

Everyone knows "unique" is code among friends for "weird," "freakish," and even just plain "fucked up,"
so, as a good friend, I wouldn't call him "unique."

MONICA

Or, I could have just meant that he was unique…You read into things too much, Frank.

FRANK

We both know that's not true.

MONICA

Alright! Fine, *fine.* I meant weirdo, freak, pretentious….

(Checking her watch.)

Tardy!

FRANK

(Smiling.)

I can't believe you said *unique.*

MONICA

(Rolling her eyes to Frank. Checking her watch.)

Damnit, Jackson…

(Looking at him waiting for an answer.)

Frank?

FRANK

Call him?

MONICA

Does he even own a cell phone?

FRANK

No.

MONICA

Then why-

FRANK

Formality.

MONICA

Of course.

(A pause.)

Oh, God! No, *NO*...Frank!

FRANK

(Laughing at her sudden outburst, mimicking her.)

Monica!

MONICA

You-You're still having him give that guest lecture, aren't you?

FRANK

Why not? He's perfect...um...fine. A lecture on *modern* art? Currently, It's *modern* times. And he's an *artist*.

MONICA

Fine. I just don't usually equate Jackson with someone who's *perfect,* or even fine, for the forming of young minds...

FRNAK

Well, When I talk to the guy who runs the class I'll tell him that.

MONICA

No, no. Don't let me stop you...

FRANK

Like you could refrain from...

10

(She cuts him off.)

MONICA

Frank, this is your *job*. It's your duty as an academic to bring in people who
are *professionals…role models…Jackson* is…

FRANK

(Coolly.)

Giving the lecture.

MONICA

Fine! Fine. Don't say I didn't warn you.

FRANK

Thanks for the warning, but I'm confidently versed on ways of bribing Jackson. He'll do fine.

MONICA

Well, just hope he shows up on time for you because…

*(Jackson runs in wearing paint coated jeans and a ripped shirt. He carries an over-stuffed shoulder bag decorated with
various scribbles and patches.)*

Glad you could join us Jackson.

JACKSON

Frank, Clock me! Early right?

FRANK

(chuckling.)

Ask Monica…

JACKSON

(Smiling.)

Early?

MONICA

Late. Very late.

JACKSON

But I-

MONICA

Shh! Late. And this...

(She gestures to his clothes.)

Joking right?

JACKSON

Yea, my real clothes are in the bag.

MONICA

(perking up.)

Really?

JACKSON

No.

MONICA

Alright...

(Breathing deeply.)

Breathe...10...9...8...7...Fuck! Buddha or Muhammad, Dr. Phil...whoever thought this shit works was high or drugged or... I-I'm going to my quiet place...

(A breath, another sudden outburst.)

Jackson, the hair, is something living in there?

FRANK

I have a comb.

JACKSON

Great! Do you keep it where your dick used to be?

FRANK

Let me guess: You left yours at *work*?

JACKSON

Fuck you.

FRANK

Don't insult my comb…It's unbreakable.

MONICA

Alright…

(She brushes off Jackson's clothes, trying to improve his appearance.)

Yea…There's hope for this…right?

FRANK

Wrong…

(Frank notices Jackson making a face at him.)

What?

JACKSON

Just thinking: The dick-less man…My god, Frank. You could nude model for undergrads! Everyone at that age hates painting dicks…I know I hated painting dicks…

FRANK

Were you jealous? But really. Jack, I couldn't model for anyone but you. I'm waiting for the dumpster-chic look to take off.

JACKSON

Me-*Ow*, Frank! Have you been watching Bravo?

MONICA

Girls be nice.

(Taking his bag and rifling through it.)

Ha! Here! Wear this…we can pretend we never knew what was going on under it…

(She begins tying a bandana on his head.)

JACKSON

(He swats it off.)

No. Let's just go in. If he likes me. He likes *me*.

FRANK

Poetic. Let's go in.

MONICA

But–

JACKSON

Monica.

MONICA

I–Fine.

(They begin to enter the building, but are stopped by Jackson's question.)

JACKSON

So what's this guy's name?

MONICA

George Signman. He likes *smart* art, so…be smart.

JACKSON

That's going to be hard for me?

FRANK

You keep us wondering, buddy…

JACKSON

Go watch some more fucking Bravo, Frank.

FRANK

That's all you got?

JACKSON

What? It's early.

MONICA

No, *Late.*

JACKSON

Right…

MONICA

Oh-God! Prints! Frank?

FRANK

I don't have them.

JACKSON

Lost the prints and your dick? Not a good day for you, huh, Frank?

MONICA

Jackson. Please…For the love of God, tell me that you brought some prints…

JACKSON

(Rummaging through his bag, dropping items.)

Nope…Wait…wait…No. Ha!

MONICA

Prints?

JACKSON

Nope…my favorite pen…Thought I lost it.

MONICA

I think I'm going to vomit…

(She begins taking her counted deep breaths again.)

JACKSON

Monica…

(He pulls out a black folder.)

I was just rattling the cage. Prints…right here.

MONICA

(Hugging him.)

Thank you for not being totally incompetent.

JACKSON

Aw, no problem. I even wipe my own ass now.

FRANK

Jackson Bell: Making baby-steps towards greatness…

JACKSON

One day at a time!

MONICA

You two want to hit to toddler before we go in?

JACKSON

Baby-steps, Monica. Not a marathon.

MONICA

Alright, Well, take some baby-steps *inside* the building.

(Lights fade on area. When they return Jackson stands at a podium in a classroom. He addresses the audience who act as the students of the classroom. Frank leans in a doorway upstage of Jackson as he speaks.)

SCENE TWO

JACKSON

Sometimes I wonder what I can get by with people like you. What won't you spend hundreds on? What do I need to smear across a canvas for you to say, "No, no, now that's *not* art." Maybe I should try facieses…Actually no, no…yes that's been done. Yes, African art made from shit. I mean really guys…Where are your standards? I don't care what you buy, that's not the issue here, I need to eat, I need to pay my bills so fucking hell, buy it. What I care about is where we draw the line. Art was holy. Portraits of kings…beautiful woman, the most beautiful in the fucking world. Christ it used to be provocative. It used to make people think, wonder, stare…It was glory…now it's fucking soup cans. Soup cans. Shit people. This is my life! My *life*, I went to school, and put my soul out there and you're out there buying soup cans and poop. Soup and poop, soup and poop…Rolls off the fucking tongue. Sometimes I think art's dead. You know how people say everything's been done? That can't be true! If everything hasn't been *lived*, then everything hasn't been *done*. Humanity doesn't exist for a god or because some monkey decided to scratch its ass standing upright; it exists to create and push forward. To make art! If it's all been done, break out the rat poison and let me make myself a fucking martini 'cus I'm done. Look around. The sky in winter is art. An elderly woman is art. Your son is art. I am art. You, you, you and you, art. Blood dripping from a cut and darkness in the furthest depths of a cave…after you turn off the flash light. Art. Soup cans, not art. Soup cans haven't been lived. They are still in the can…unopened. I am opened. I'm lived, and you are too. Don't let them sell you something that's unopened and let them say it's art! Art is every single one of us, and for someone to say we're still on the shelf. Well, shit, it's wrong. Even if I tired I couldn't stay on the shelf. Doesn't he think I've tired? My first reaction upon exiting the womb wasn't, "Mom I think I am going to choose a career path that almost surely guarantees me I will be working in an apron and pointed paper hat." People don't choose to jump of the shelf into poverty, cancer, lost love, crushed dreams, long days at work, an angry teenager that *used* to be your biggest fan, a disappointed father who looks at you like you let him down…on purpose. If I could choose to stay on the shelf, pristine and unopened that's where I'd be. That's where we'd all be. But people have to live, get their Campbell's label ripped off, dints in their can, be opened and drained empty…

(A bell dismissing the class tolls 5 PM.)

And get the fuck out…I think you for what I am sure was your undivided attention, especially the gentleman in the back who was kind enough to offer his neighbor mouth to mouth recitation.

(Frank comes forward and places a hand on Jackson's shoulder.)

FRANK

Thanks for coming.

JACKSON

Thanks for the effort, Frank, but I don't think I'm a very captivating teacher.

FRANK

You should see the days I lecture, a kid in the front actually brings a pillow…

JACKSON

I was just ripped apart by a bunch of undergrads.

FRANK

Don't feel bad, last week it was poor Monet…and the poor fuck wasn't even here to defend himself.

(Jackson laughs.)

JACKSON

So, are you free now, or do you have some parent teacher conference or…

FRANK

Come on, I'll buy you some coffee.

JACKSON

I'll buy yours.

(Jackson removes a newspaper clipping from his pocket and hands it to Frank.)

FRANK

Well, Fuck me, *you* sold something?

JACKSON

Hard to believe, isn't it? Look at the name, Frankie.

FRANK

George Signman? Aw, Well, Monica will be proud.

JACKSON

Guy's a real class act, Frank. I mean you drop off the prints…do the whole meet and greet…Don't expect these people to actually show up at the show…but I'm standing there at the door after my show ends, people running for the exit, you know the usual reactions…and here comes George, check in hand, and says in that ever so classic voice, shit, Frank that voice…

FRANK

I know, you laughed in his face when he introduced himself…

JACKSON

Well, you or Monica should have warned me…

FRANK

Sorry. Didn't know I'd need to tell you not to laugh in the face of a potential employer.

JACKSON

Uh, that would be a *current* employer, thank you. Alright so, after the show, people are making their exodus, and here comes George…voice and all…

(Imitating the voice.)

"Excuse me, sir. You are the artist, correct." I'm a little scared, I think he wants to punch me or something…I mean that's usually the case, but he gives me the check, right? And he says, "I do hope this is not an offensive amount, Mr. Bell." Mr. fucking Bell, right? So, I look at this check, 5,000 dollars, Frank. I think Ol' George wants to buy the whole gallery, turns out he wanted one painting. One painting. So, I sold it. Something about him…I like him. Turns out he's doing this private owner show of his famous collection…and. Drum roll, Frank…

(Frank half-heartedly drums with a pen on the podium.)

He's featuring my painting. I think he liked me, Frank

FRANK

Incredible, Jack. I'll buy you dinner.

JACKSON

I'll buy *you* dinner.

FRANK

Alright Trump, we'll see when get there.

JACKSON

I'll rock, paper, scissors, your ass. In front of people…Don't make me go there, Frank. I'll go.

FRANK

What are you, five?

JACKSON

What are you, an art teacher? Shit…you are. I'm sorry man, that sucks.

FRANK

Come on, let's eat…

JACKSON

Aw, I hurt your feelings, didn't I?

FRANK

No, I just made myself sad when I thought about what you were, unemployed.

JACKSON

I'd be hurt, but I know you are only lashing out due to the frustration you harbor from having to go to your horrifically dead-end-job…day after day…

(Jackson puts his arm around Frank.)

I know it's hard for you. But just know…just know I'm here for you, Frank.

FRANK

Must you be so much like *you*…all the time?

JACKSON

Unfortunately…

FRANK

That must be rough.

JACKSON

God, Frank, and what does it say about you…You *choose* to spend your time with me. You're a sick bastard, Frank.

FRANK

(Pushing Jackson to the exit.)

A hungry one, too…

JACKSON

This one's on you, right?

FRANK

After all that…I mean, you just…yeah. Sure, my fucking treat.

SCENE THREE

(Lights go down on area, when they return, Frank and Jackson sit in a dinner booth, joined by Monica.)

JACKSON

…And this old fucker comes up and there's this check in his hand, right?

FRANK

Do the voice…

JACKSON

I am…Jesus calm down, Frank.

FRANK

Sorry.

JACKSON

Comes up to me with the check, and just take a guess who it is Monica…

MONICA

Bob Ross?

JACKSON

(Pulling the newspaper article from his pocket.)

Bam! It would be a Mr. George Signman.

MONICA

(She takes the article, shocked.)

He likes you?

JACKSON

Oh, I think its love, Mon'.

MONICA

Wow. Do go on…

JACKSON

So here he comes. And you know, he's got *the voice*…

FRANK

Best part…

JACKSON

Shut the fuck up, Frank…

FRANK

Fine…

JACKSON

Walks right up, hands me the check and says,

(Imitating the voice.)

"I hope this isn't an offensive amount, Mr. Bell…"

FRANK

(Motioning to Jackson.)

Mr. Bell?

JACKSON

Frank!

FRANK

Sorry…Christ.

JACKSON

And that was that…He buys the painting…

FRANK

One painting…

JACKSON

Fucking 5,000 dollars! So—

(Taking a cell phone from his pocket and tossing it onto the table.)

I got one of these.

MONICA

That's great, Peacock.

(A beat.)

JACKSON

One: Don't call me Peacock. Two: Spill it. What's wrong with you? The real Monica would have had a delightfully evil rip at my character and abilities there…and all you did was say 'That's great, Peacock.' Something must be wrong. Come on Monica, insult me…I'm scared.

FRANK

You have seemed a bit muted, Mon'.

MONICA

(Pathetically trying to play along.)

I'm sorry boys…I didn't want to bring you down Jackson…You seemed so comfortable up there…on your high horse.

JACKSON

That was a *little* better, but not quite as biting as the Monica I've come to hate so much.

MONICA

They're closing my gallery. Daddy's gallery…

FRANK

What?

MONICA

I was doing the books and…we're bankrupt. All my investors think it's best to just close… Seeing that I've been on a study decline for the past few years now…

FRANK

Monica…I'm so sorry. You love that place.

MONICA

Loved, Frank. That gallery was dad's life, and I take over and it's…over…God-I killed my dad's baby…

JACKSON

First off, you're your dad's baby. Nothing you can do will change that. Second, stop worrying. I'm sure that Frank and I can figure out something. With his brains and my dashing charm…surely we can do…something…

MONICA

(Monica smiles.)

Thanks, but I don't think there's anything even your charm can do, Peacock…

JACKSON

(A little hurt.)

What about Frank's brains?

FRANK

I don't think so, Jack…

JACKSON

I want to help…

MONICA

I know, Peacock…

(She pats his head and stands to go.)

I've got to get to the gallery…start moving my things…Bye boys. Sorry I rained on your parade Jackson…

JACKSON

Rain on my parade? Are people our age even allowed to say that?

MONICA

Got me—I'm old.

JACKSON

Monica…I'm…sorry.

(She smiles and exits. Frank looks Jackson over and laughs.)

What?

FRANK

I don't know; I just find your tragic flirting humorous.

JACKSON

Fuck. Frank what's wrong with me? Monica? I might as well want to date my sister…

FRANK

You've known her since you were what? 12?…Maybe it just took you a while to realize she's *not* your sister…and that you *can* date her.

25

JACKSON

(Hitting his head into the table.)

She thinks I'm ridiculous, Frank…She loves to laugh at me…It's what we do. And now here I am, completely serious about her…and to her I'm still a joke.

FRANK

You are a joke. But you're a good joke. Just see what happens.

JACKSON

Keep flirting?

FRANK

If you want to stay friends…

JACKSON

Fuck you.

FRANK

Kidding. I'm sure you'll marry and have fifty angry little art kids…all of them just as quirky as you and as high-strung as Monica.

JACKSON

(Smiles weakly.)

Thanks.

FRANK

Don't mention it…

JACKSON

So…Any romance in your forecast, Frank?

FRANK

No time for it.

JACKSON

(Cheekily.)

There's always time for love, Frank.

FRANK

Maybe for you…I've got a job…and

JACKSON

And what? I bet Monica has other friends, Frank. Lady friends…Art lovers…See where I'm going?

FRANK

Perfectly, now stop.

JACSKON

I'm trying to look out for you, Frank. What about a student? There's got to be that one little slut that has that teacher lovin' thing going on…huh?

FRANK

You're ill.

JACKSON

Right…That's not really your style…It's more me…You know, Frank, you're making this very hard on me.

FRANK

I'm going for impossible.

JACKSON

I don't believe in the impossible. We're getting you a girl…or what have you…

FRANK

Whoa, What's the supposed to mean?

JACKSON

Didn't want to narrow your horizons, Frank. I think that coffee refill guy obviously has a thing for you…He really cares about how much sugar you take…

FRANK

He cares about his tip, not my sugar.

JACKSON

He defiantly cares about *your sugar.*

FRANK

Sugar or not. You aren't hooking me up with any girl or…what have you.

JACKSON

You're just saying that because you're nervous. And— You know you can't get girl or what have you without me.

FRANK

If I wanted a girl, I'd get her…

JACKSON

(Interjecting.)

Or what have you….

FRANK

… Myself. Now stop!

JACKSON

Fine. You're a lost cause…myself, however, will be needing your undivided attention on my quest.

FRANK

Quest? Who are you?

JACKSON

Monica's knight.

FRANK

Heh, That's cute…

JACKSON

It's not cute, it's dashing.

FRANK

Uh-huh, You just make sure that you keep that up around, Monica.

JACKSON

I'm always dashing, Frank.

FRANK

Oh, is that what you call it?

JACKSON

No, It's what everyone who knows me calls it.

SCENE FOUR

(Lights fade on area, when they return Frank is in his apartment on the phone, he talks to his brother, Martin.)

FRANK

Tomorrow…Martin…Well, that's fucking great Martin, give me a lot of time here. I know…

(Jackson walks in and motions to Frank to ask who it is, Frank mimes various mocks of Martin to Jackson, who laughs.)

Yes. I am listening…No, I didn't laugh, I have company.

JACKSON

Company…

FRANK

Martin says, Hi. And he wants you to get a real job.

(Jackson takes the phone from Frank.)

JACKSON

You want me to get a job Marty? Yeah? I want you to slide your father's dick out of your ass but we can't all have what we want.

(Jackson hangs up the phone.)

So, Why are you ruining my week with *Martin?*

FRANK

He's moving…and the house isn't ready yet, and he needs a place for the week.

JACKSON

And he needs your place?

(Frank nods. Jackson begins eating a bowl a nuts sitting on Frank's coffee table.)

You know, Frank, you should really stop letting people walk all over you. Who the fuck does he think he is? Just barging in here…

FRANK

Right…

JACKSON

You should have just told him 'No. Martin, I'm a busy man, and you can't barge in here, expecting me to be free, with no plans, ready to entertain you."

(Jackson eats a handful of nuts.)

FRANK

He is my brother, If I can do something I should, right?

JACKSON

Wrong! Your brother is Martin. Martin is bad. Therefore your brother is bad.

FRANK

He's not that bad.

JACKSON

Right, and Attila the Hun was a misunderstood teddy-bear.

FRANK

Come on, Jack…

JACKSON

(Eating more nuts.)

So how is Attila?

FRANK

Promoted. He's Dad's new spread designer…

JACKSON

I'd be impressed…But…

FRANK

You know him, right…It must be nice to have it handed all to you…

JACKSON

(Eating more nuts.)

I know, right?

FRANK

Right…

JACKSON

So…Attila is here for how long?

FRANK

'Till Monday…

JACKSON

Great. See you Monday.

FRANK

You can't just leave me alone with him…that long.

JACKSON

Oh, but I can. I'm working on this thing, where I don't let myself feel guilt…It's an ancient technique, all the Chinese gurus did it…So, Sorry, Frank.

FRNAK

Fine… 'Till Monday.

JACKSON

Any word on Mon's gallery?

FRNAK

None.

JACKSON

I'm not going to let her lose that space, Frank.

FRANK

She wanted to buy the building, but the down payment is just too much…

JACKSON

How much?

FRANK

15 grand.

JACKSON

Shit…

FRANK

(Frank smiles.)

You've got it bad, Sir knight.

JACKSON

You don't think I can do the Camelot bit, do you?

FRANK

You need a stallion and a lance. Then I'd believe you.

JACKSON

Start believing, Frank. I'll get fucking 30 grand…She's keeping that gallery

FRANK

Lunch tomorrow?

JACKSON

Martin will be attending this lunch, no?

FRANK

I assume I should feed him…

JACKSON

Are you sure? Do demons eat? We should look into that, I'm mean, if not we might be able to get away with locking him in a closet somewhere…

FRANK

He's coming, Jack. Are you?

JACKSON

With Martin? Me, Martin lunch, public locations…your tendency to embarrass easily? Are any of these adding up to you?

FRANK

I'll call Monica…

JACKSON

You know…Martin's really not *that* bad. I'll be there.

FRANK

Thank you.

JACKSON

Don't thank me, thank Monica. Well, I've got some planning to do.

FRANK

Planning?

JACKSON

I've got to go get knighted before lunch tomorrow.

FRANK

(Frank laughs.)

Alright. Until tomorrow.

JACKSON

Good morrow, squire.

FRANK

(Frank rolls his eyes.)

Leave.

JACKSON

(Making a grand bow.)

Adieu.

SCENE FIVE

(Jackson exits, the lights fade on the area, when they return Frank and Jackson have returned to the diner accompanied with Martin.)

JACKSON

Frank…

FRANK

I'm sorry. I don't know why she would be late.

JACKSON

I'm not here to eat with bozo here.

MARTIN

Aw, fuck you.

JACKSON

Creative, real creative.

MARTIN

So, asshole, what do you even do with your life anymore?

JACKSON

Let me give you a break down: I sleep until about noon, wake up, take a shit, think about how I hate you, paint greatness, take another shit, create some more greatness, get myself off to some Picasso to top off the evening, and then off to bed.

MARTIN

Sounds like you're really useful to the world.

JACKSON

Let me hear about your day. Really interested. How does a real man, like yourself, get through the day?

MARTIN

I started with getting a job…

JACKSON

From dad…Good.

MARTIN

Least it's a job…

JACKSON

Uh-huh. A job, where you bend over your desk, spread your legs, and get fucked by the corporate man. Please continue…

MARTIN

You…just fuck off.

JACKSON

Again, the linguistic skills of a Harvard grad. Listen to your brother, Frank. He's damn near fucking Einstein.

MARTIN

If you're so fucking smart then why can't you get a job?

JACKSON

You see, You can't change the fact that you are stupid. I *can* get a job, I *choose* to not. Unfortunately, you *can't* be intelligent. Did you get all that? It's a *paradox,* isn't it Martin…Oh, And, Martin. I almost forgot, I've got something for you.

(Jackson ruffles through his bad finding some pastels and chalk.)

Here ya' go, Marty…You can draw on your napkin. Can you draw me a kitty?

MARTIN

I'll draw you a big glass of shut the fuck up!

JACKSON

And a kitty?

MARTIN

(Picking up a pastel.)

You know how many places this would fit in your body?

JACKSON

Ohh, Scary!

(Monica enters hurriedly and sits at the table.)

MONICA

Sorry boys. I got held up at the gallery.

JACKSON

Oh—

MARTIN

(*Running his eyes up and down Monica.*)

Hey…Don't be sorry…

JACKSON

Why don't you just ask her to take off her top?

MARTIN

Grow up.

(*Martin smiles at Monica.*)

He can be a bit much, I'm sure *you* know that.

JACKSON

Go push a fourth grader, boost your fucking ego…

MONICA

Jackson, be nice. Hi, you must be Martin.

(*They shake hands.*)

MARTIN

(*Hitting Jackson in the back of the head.*)

Like a puppy, you just gotta rub his nose in the piddle 'till he learns.

(*Monica laughs. Jackson opens his mouth ready to protest.*)

And you are?

MONICA

Right, Sorry! I'm Monica. Monica Graham…

MARTIN

A pleasure…

JACKSON

You...fucking...

FRANK

(Cutting Jackson off.)

Should we order? I think I'm going to have the soup. Martin, soup? Anyone? Jackson, you like soup, right? So who's getting soup?

MONICA

Soup sounds nice.

JACKSON/MARTIN

It does!

(Jackson and Martin glare at each other.)

JACKSON

How are you Monica?

MONICA

I'm coping...

MARTIN

Oh, is something wrong?

JACKSON

You fucking ass...

FRANK

(Aside to Jackson.)

Not really...knightly, Jack.

MONICA

Well, I own a gallery. It's my family's, well It's mine now...Was mine. Long story short It's bankrupt so...

(She shrugs, defeated.)

MARTIN

I'm terribly sorry to hear that.

JACKSON

I bet you are. Martin have you ever seen a painting?

MONICA

Jackson! Would you stop?

JACKSON

(Hurt.)

Monica…I

MARTIN

Honestly, maybe you should excuse yourself and let the big kids eat.

(Monica laughs.)

JACKSON

If I saw any here, I would.

FRANK

(To himself.)

This is going great.

MARTIN

So, Mrs. Graham…

MONICA

Ms…And please, Just Monica.

MARTIN

Of course, *Ms.* Have long have you…been in the acquaintance of my brother?

JACKSON

That's not even proper syntax.

FRANK

Jack…

MARTIN

You've known Frank, long?

MONICA

Since undergrad…Jackson- since middle school.

MARTIN

I didn't ask about our friend in his terrible twos…Jackson, please, if you are going to play with you crayons…pick them up.

(Martin gathers the pastels and hands them to Jackson, who places them back in his sack. Monica laughs.)

MONICA

Frank, you never told me your brother was so…funny.

MARTIN

Oh, Well, Frank just doesn't want me upstaging him…Well, you've been quiet Jackson, don't you have anything witty to add?

(He laughs.)

JACKSON

I…You know…I'm not really hungry anymore…Bye Monica…Frank…

(Jackson exits.)

FRANK

(After a pause.)

Soup?

MONICA

What was with him? He was worse than usual.

FRANK

I didn't notice a difference.

MONICA

Oh, come on, Frank! Don't excuse him. He was being incredibly rude to your brother.

MARTIN

Oh, don't feel bad, Honey. That's just Jackson.

MONICA

(Monica smiles.)

Just Jackson…

FRANK

Yeah.

MONICA

Frank, what soup are you getting?

(Frank, looking out the window, fails to respond.)

MONICA

Frank?

FRANK

Oh, broccoli…

MONICA

Frank, are you alright?

FRANK

Yea…yea…I'm fine.

(Putting on his best smile.)

Let's eat.

MONICA

Honey, what's wrong?

FRANK

Just tired.

MARTIN

(Attempting to sound compassionate.)

Poor Frank, has to face those spoiled college brats every day…Poor guy must be tired.

(Frank rolls his eyes.)

MONICA

So, What do you do, Martin?

MARTIN

I work for our father. We run a small sports magazine…I design the spreads.

MONICA

Wow, two artists in the family.

MARTIN

Aw, well, Frank's the real creative mind in the family. Honestly, I don't know a thing about art…I just put the pictures on the page.

FRANK

(Mumbling to himself.)

And even that's an overstatement…

MARTIN

What was that?

FRANK

Just asking who's ready to order…

(Lights fade on area. When they return Martin is pacing around Frank's apartment. Frank sits at the kitchen table, reading the paper.)

MARTIN

Alright, that's it! You're helping me.

FRANK

With what?

MARTIN

Getting on your cute friend's good side.

FRANK

No, no, Martin…You're not that big of a jerk are you? Can't you see Jackson obviously has feelings for her?

MARTIN

Well, are they a thing?

FRANK

Not yet…

MARTIN

Then fuck Jackson! Alright, This is what we are going to do: I'm going to get girly her gallery. That will so get me in the door…

FRANK

Martin, do you just have 15 thousand dollars lying around?

MARTIN

The fuck?

FRANK

Then you're not getting her the gallery.

MARTIN

Help me think.

FRANK

Help you think? There is nothing to think about. You aren't doing anything…anything with Monica.

MARTIN

Correction, *Jackson's* not doing anything with Monica…

(Martin laughs.)

FRANK

I'm not doing this with you.

MARTIN

Listen Frankie…If I get the girl, Jackson is what?

FRANK

What are you talking about?

MARTIN

He's?

FRANK

…What?

MARTIN

Single. And you're…

FRANK

I'm what, Martin?

MARTIN

Drop the act, bro…You have been sportin' a bone for him since college.

FRANK

I'm not 'sporting a bone' for anyone…

MARTIN

Drop it Frank. I'm your brother, I've got you all figured out…

FRANK

(Frank sighs.)

You've got me figured out?

(Martin nods.)

Alright. Fine, Martin. What do you want to keep quiet?

MARTIN

Frank, you make me sound like a monster. All I want is some help with Monica.

FRANK

No. I'm not going to do that to Jack…

MARTIN

Aw, that's really fucking sweet, Frank. Stand up for your man…But I don't give shit about your brotherly love, so, are you in or out?

FRANK

Out.

MARTIN

More ways than one.

(Martin pulls his cell phone from his pocket.)

FRANK

Whoa, wait what are you doing?

MARTIN

I'm just going to put in a little call to your boy toy…

FRANK

Martin…We aren't teenagers anymore. You aren't really…

(Martin is holding the phone to his ear.)

Fuck.

MARTIN

Jackson? Hey, there…Now, now, now that's a bit rude…

(Frank frantically nods to Martin.)

Just wanted to tell you that…Monica deserves a man and that man is me. Bye now.

(Martin hangs up the phone.)

FRANK

You are probably the worst human being I know.

MARTIN

Don't over-exaggerate, Frankie.

FRANK

Fine Martin. But if I help you, you won't say anything about…

MARTIN

How you're a fag?

FRANK

How I…*feel*…about Jackson?

MARTIN

Not a word.

FRANK

Alright…Well, We are defiantly going to have to class you up…

MARTIN

Right. Give me some lines about your art crap. She likes that, right?

FRANK

She does own an *art* gallery…Shit…This is going to be impossible.

MARTIN

Nothing's impossible. I just need a bit of…a queer eye…

(*Martin laughs at his own joke.*)

FRANK

You're an ass.

MARTIN

That hurts a little, from my own brother.

FRANK

Can't you busy yourself with something, anything else…

(*Frank sighs, sits and begins to read a newspaper, Martin snatches it up and begins to read.*)

I was reading…Alright.

MARTIN

I'm busying myself…Christ! Have you seen this?

FRANK

Seen what?

MARTIN

One of Jackson's shitty paintings…sold for fucking 5K.

FRANK

Yes. He told me. What about it?

MARTIN

I don't know, I was just thinking if any of your shit would sell we could get that money.

FRANK

Well, I don't have that much shit to sell…And I don't really get the chance to paint since I've started teaching, so forget it.

MARTIN

Let's just borrow some of…Jackson's. Wait…Fuck, Frankie that's it!

FRANK

No. Stop it now. Don't think about, don't even say it.

MARTIN

Come on, he's bound to have so much shit piled up that he wouldn't even notice…Frank just go over to his place and pocket a few.

FRANK

Pocket paintings? You really are an oaf aren't you?

MARTIN

Get in there when he's not home then.

FRANK

I am absolutely not doing this.

(*Martin takes out his phone.*)

Alright! We get in there how?

MARTIN

You don't have a key or something?

FRANK

Oh, Fuck you…

MARTIN

Well?

FRANK

Oh great, now I'm planning the romantic demise of my best friend…

Martin

Get over it and think.

FRANK

He always gives me his keys if he drinks…

MARTIN

Sounds like the boys are going out tonight then…

FRANK

(Beginning to exit to his bedroom.)

You're deplorable.

MARTIN

Hey Frank, A Rabbi, a Priest and a Fairy are sitting at a bar…

FRANK

Shut up!

(Jackson bounds into the room carrying a large canvas.)

JACKSON

It's fucking brilliant, Frank!

FRANK

What's brilliant?

JACKSON

This.

(He holds the painting up for Frank to inspect.)

Well?

FRANK

Well...

(Martin looks it over quickly.)

MARTIN

Hate it.

JACKSON

I didn't ask the peanut gallery. Frank?

FRANK

I...*like* it...

JACKSON

Lie. Tell me what you really think.

FRANK

I think...

JACKSON

It's ironic Frank, beautifully ironic. Your little hellions gave me the idea. It's Warhol, it's me, it's grotesque...Frank, it's fucking brilliant...

FRANK

It's...just...Are you sure you are really in a place in your career to mock one of pop culture's most revered works?

JACKSON

Career...

MARTIN

What career?

JACKSON

...*This* is my career! Frank this is going to make me a name. I'm sure of it.

FRANK

A name?

(*Frank takes the painting from Jackson turning it for him to see, revealing the painting to the audience. It is a destroyed soup can, mocking the famous Warhols.*)

This is the name you want for yourself?

JACKSON

Frank. Let me ask you a question…

FRANK

Shoot.

JACKSON

As a blind follower of the death trap of by-the-book art…

FRANK

Fuck you…

JACKSON

No thanks. As a bland, hack, who is slave to a paint-by-numbers concept of art: Does this piss you off?

MARTIN

Yes, take your lame ass painting and leave!

JACKSON

I was talking to your brother, Peanut.

FRANK

Yes, it pisses me off.

JACKSON

Excellent, now why?

(*The two begin to circle the painting, like vultures circling a carcass.*)

MARTIN

Because you won't leave!

JACKSON

Peanut, let your brother finish...

FRANK

You can't presume to just mock people who are...

JACKSON

Were you going to say better? Or maybe more respected? What is it you said earlier? Ah, revered...

FRANK

Pick one.

JACKSON

Frank, Frank, Frank. Don't you get it? This is just what I want!

FRANK

Of course it is...

(The two go into a fast paced art argument. Martin confusedly looks between the two looking for a moment to interject.)

JACKSON

The attempt to be totally modern...

FRANK

Totally modern? You can't just forget the past! The modern can only come from what we know...

JACKSON

You're wrong! That is to say novelty is impossible. That all is based on something...

FRANK

That is exactly why technique exists.

JACKSON

It shouldn't, Frank! Don't you get it? Fuck, of course you don't, you're a fucking teacher. You are only furthering this asinine ideal that is aiming to destroy novelty for those of us…

FRANK

Fine! Why don't you experiment with…

JACKSON

I do not experiment!

FRANK

Your palate seems over-saturated is all I was saying…

JACKSON

Over-saturated? Over-saturated! Your fucking opinion of the grandiose idea of *technique* is what is over-saturated here…

MARTIN

(Yelling over the two.)

So…Who wants a beer?

JACKSON

What?

MARTIN

Come on, Boys night out…Have a few drinks, find a few ladies…

(Looking at Frank.)

Or what have you…

JACKSON

What have you…

MARTIN

See, your little peon wants to go…

JACKSON

Now, What makes you think that I would ever spend recreational time with you?

MARTIN

Frank…

(Frank catches on to Martin's plan.)

FRANK

Come on Jack, it could be…fun.

JACKSON

And Chinese water torture *can* be relaxing…Bye Frank. Me and my genius are leaving…

(Jackson picks up his painting preparing to leave.)

FRANK

Jackson!

(Martin looks to Frank, shrugging. Frank pulls Jackson downstage to converse away from Martin.)

Don't make me do this alone…

JACKSON

I told you about my no guilt thing, Right? The gurus? Ancient techniques?

FRANK

Listen, I will personally work my charms on Monica…*for you,* if you go.

JACKSON

Frank. You have no charms.

FRANK

You go tonight…all our tabs are paid. You owe me nothing.

JACKSON

Huh. Alright. How much do I owe you?

FRANK

I stopped adding…

JACKSON

Alright. For you, Frank, I'll go.

FRANK

Really?

JACKSON

Yes. Get ape boy ready, I'll drop off my masterpiece…Fuck, I hate you.

FRANK

Thanks, Jack.

JACKSON

Yea, Yea…

(Jackson exits.)

MARTIN

Well?

FRANK

He's coming…

MARTIN

Phase one…

FRANK

I feel sick…

MARTIN

You'll get over that…

SCENE SEVEN

(Lights fade on area when they return they are in Jackson's flat, Jackson is drunk Frank and Martin carry him in.)

JACKSON

And another thing…Fuck museums…fuck the whole goddamn system…I don't need it. I'm doin' fine. You hear that MO.M.A? FINE!

FRANK

Aw, you tell 'em, Jack. Come here. Sit down.

JACKSON

I'm great…I…

(Jackson stumbles.)

Whoa. Sitting is *good*.

MARTIN

So…where'd you put your keys, Jack?

JACKSON

Somewhere…table…

FRANK

Smooth, Martin.

MARTIN

What? He's shit-canned. He won't remember a thing.

JACKSON

Frank. Sit with me. I have to tell you something.

FRANK

(Frank sits beside Jackson, lies him down and puts a blanket over him.)

What?

JACKSON

(Jackson sits up, pushing off the blanket and whispers, loudly.)

I have an extra nipple, Frank. Who will ever love me? Not Monica…She's a high class lady…High class ladies don't like freaks…I'm a freak, Frank…

(Martin laughs.)

FRANK

You're not a freak…Wait, you really have…

JACKSON

Yes! It looks like a freckle…but…it's not. Totally a nipple.

FRANK

Get some rest, alright, Jack?

JACKSON

I'll show you, Frank. I'll show you 'cus I trust you

(Jackson lifts his shirt. Martin begins to search the apartment.)

JACKSON

Frank, Frank, see? Right here. Weird huh?

FRANK

Yeah…Put your shirt down…

MARTIN

Why Frank? You getting hot and bothered?

FRANK

I *hate* you.

JACKSON

Heh…*Everyone* hates Martin. I know I do. Martin, did I ever tell you that? I *hate* you…

MARTIN

That's great, dude. I feel the same way about you.

JACKSON

We bonded, Frank.

FRANK

That's…great, Jack.

JACKSON

Uh-oh…

FRANK

What?

(Jackson holds his stomach and moans.)

Oh. *Uh-oh*…Trash can?

JACKSON

Please.

FRANK

Martin. Trash can…

MARTIN

(Looking around for the can.)

Where the fuck…

(He finds a bowl lying on the kitchenette.)

Here.

(He brings it over closer to Jackson, who bends over, aiming for the bowl, but vomits on Martin's shoe. Martin rubs it off on Jackson's couch.)

Shit! God damn…little…

FRANK

You deserve that.

MARTIN

Probably…

JACKSON

I'm better now.

FRANK

Good.

(Martin resumes his search of the flat, finally finding the keys.)

MARTIN

Got 'em!

FRANK

Thank God. Jack? You okay?

MARTIN

Fuck him, let's go.

JACKSON

I like you…Look at your funny glasses…

(Jackson takes Frank's glasses and puts them on.)

I'm teacher, Frank.

FRANK

Funny. Alright, Jack…I need those…

(Jackson returns the glasses to Frank.)

Thanks.

(Jackson pinches Frank's nose.)

JACKSON

Got your nose…

(Jackson lies back and closes his eyes.)

FRANK

You can keep that…

(Jackson giggles.)

You have the keys?

(Martin reveals the keys.)

Let's go.

JACKSON

'Night Frank! I'll keep your nose safe.

FRANK

Thanks, Jack. 'Night…

JACKSON

You're a good guy, ya' know that, Frank?

FRANK

(Sighing.)

Thanks…

JACKSON

Frank's my best friend…he looks out for me…right nose?

(Doing a voice for the nose.)

That's right Jackson!

FRANK

Just…Go to bed, Jack.

SCENE EIGHT

(Lights fade on area. The scene opens with Frank and Monica sitting in the diner.)

FRANK

Even though it was a forced outing…This was nice.

MONICA

Well, I was getting concerned…

FRANK

Alive and well…

MONICA

So, Have you seen the new masterpiece?

FRANK

The soup can?

MONICA

That's the one…

FRANK

What do you think?

MONICA

Well…It's very Jackson…

FRANK

Pollock or Bell?

MONICA

You're lucky he's not here…He hates Pollock.

FRANK

He hates his name.

MONICA

He's toying around with "Demetri" again…

FRANK

Wonderful…

MONICA

(Laughing.)

He's so…ridiculous. *Actually* trying to change his name. Ridiculous!

FRANK

Now, be nice…

MONICA

I will when he does! The way he treated your brother…

FRANK

Right, what do you care about my brother?

MONICA

I…

FRANK

Monica, You *don't*

MONICA

God! No. He's nice, Frank, but…no.

FRANK

Good to hear, you have about as much in common with him as I do…

MONICA

Changing the subject….Jackson tells me that you are in love.

FRANK

What?

MONICA

He says he tried to set you up and...

FRANK

And what? Because I didn't want *Jackson* setting me up...I'm in love?

MONICA

It's what he thinks...

FRANK

(Trying to laugh it off, but obviously shaken.)

Heh...Well, Let him think it...

(A pause.)

MONICA

Alright, enough skirting the issue. Frank. What's wrong?

FRANK

Wrong? That's low, Monica, I come here to have lunch with my friend...and now that I'm here you're...

MONICA

Frank. It's me. I've known you for 12 years. I know when something's wrong, when you are lying, and I know that when Jackson's caught on to something being wrong, it's serious. So, let's hear it.

FRANK

(Sigh.)

Jack-

MONICA

Oh no, what did he do now?

FRANK

-Nothing!

MONICA

Then I'm having a hard time seeing the problem…

FRANK

Alright. From the beginning.

MONICA

A good place to start…

FRANK

Cute. Let's see…Fuck. Alright…Alright, here we go. Um, You remember when you set me up with your roommate in school?

MONICA

And she left before dinner was over?

FRANK

Right, through the window, over a dumpster, ran through the woods… Monica, Do you know why she left?

MONICA

She said you

(Mocking the girl.)

'Weren't into her…'

FRANK

I wasn't. She leaned in and was waiting for me to…kiss her. And I just let her…sit there bent across the table, eyes closed…

MONICA

(Broadly smiling, understanding him, but playing along.)

Gosh. Why Frank?

FRANK

I found nothing about her attractive.

MONICA

(Nearly laughing.)

It was her glasses, wasn't it? Frank. I never had you pegged to be so shallow, but you are a man…I don't know why I'm surprised…

FRANK

It wasn't her glasses, Monica. I'm…

MONICA

Gay?

FRANK

I'm…What did you say?

MONICA

I said you're gay.

FRANK

You know?

MONICA

(Leaning over the table whispering.)

Even coffee guy knows.

FRANK

Jackson knows?

MONICA

(Whispering again.)

Jackson knows.

(A pause.)

FRANK

Well, Surprise…

MONICA

(Laughing.)

12 years honey! We may be socially-dense artists…but give us *some* credit.

FRANK

Why didn't you two ever say anything?

MONICA

We figured we'd let you do the talking. Didn't figure it would take this long…

FRANK

What, did you two meet?

MONICA

Yes, twice a week. Frank, don't make a big deal of it. We didn't.

FRANK

Well, sorry, Monica…I'm just wrapping my mind around the fact that I was the only one I was fooling…

MONICA

So, we knew. That's been the looming, terrible thing bothering you, huh?

FRANK

It's deeper than that, Mon'.

MONICA

Deeper?

FRANK

A bit more complicated…

MONICA

Complicated?

FRANK

Are you doing that on purpose?

MONICA

Purpose?

FRANK

Monica-

MONICA

Sorry, honey, this is just a bit boring…You were saying?

FRANK

(Taking in a deep breath and speaking quickly.)

I…think I have feelings for Jackson.

MONICA

(Screaming.)

What?

FRANK

Shit! Monica, my ears…

MONICA

Sorry. You *think*?

FRANK

I know. I've known, I loose sleep…Happy?

MONICA

(Laughing.)

A little.

FRANK

You're a sick bitch, aren't you?

MONICA

I think it's adorable.

FRANK

Adorable…

MONICA

Yes, Frank. It's adorable in every way…But…

FRANK

I know.

MONICA

You have to tell him.

FRANK

Wow, Monica. You think of that all by yourself? Glad I brought the issue to you…

MONICA

Well, Shit, Frank, I don't know. Maybe you can turn him…

FRANK

Turn him? Did you really just say that?

MONICA

You're right, Frank. Absolutely, right. There is no hope. Is that better? What do I say?

FRANK

(Near a whisper.)

I don't know…

MONICA

I'm sorry.

FRANK

Yeah…

MONICA

(Smiling.)

Frank…

FRANK

What?

MONICA

(Taking his hand from across the table.)

I still think it's adorable.

FRANK

Fuck you.

(Both laugh. Martin enters the diner, looking around. He spots Monica and Frank and makes his way to them.)

MARTIN

What's so funny?

(The two smile to each other but don't respond.)

Alright. I get it. *Girl* talk…

(Frank rolls his eyes. Martin turns to Monica.)

I thought I'd find you here. I woke up and Frankie was already gone…

MONICA

My fault. I called him for brunch.

MARTIN

Brunch. Sweet…

FRANK

Martin. What do you want?

MARTIN

I woke up this morning and I was thinking to myself, 'Martin, that Monica seems like a wonderful and charming woman and it would be a true shame if she lost that gallery…'

FRANK

And?

MARTIN

(Martin pulls a check from his jacket pocket.)

This is for you, Ms. Graham.

MONICA

For-

(She looks at the check.)

No…Martin I can't take this…

MARTIN

Well, It wasn't selfless. I was thinking you could pay me back…

MONICA

Oh?

MARTIN

Go to dinner with me tonight?

MONICA

That's so…But still, I can't take this.

MARTIN

You give that to me, and I will hand it to the homeless man I passed on the corner. I want you to have it. Dinner?

FRANK

(*To himself.*)

Christ…

MONICA

Yes.

MARTIN

Yes, you'll take the money?

MONICA

No, yes to diner. Here, take your check.

MARTIN

That bum is really going to be happy…

FRANK

Just take it, Mon'.

MARTIN

Please?

MONICA

Well…

FRANK

(*Taking the check from Martin, Giving it to Monica.*)

She'll take the damn money!

MONICA

Frank…

MARTIN

Glad to hear it. I'll pick you up at 8?

MONICA

Sure…

MARTIN

See you at 8…

MONICA

See you…

(Martin exits. Monica stares down at the check. A long pause.)

Shit, honey, what were we talking about?

FRANK

Never mind.

SCENE NINE

(Lights come up on area. The sound of a phone ringing is heard. Jackson still sleeps on his couch. He stirs hearing the phone and digs through the blanket retrieving the phone. He answers.)

JACKSON

What? Oh! Yes, sir…I…What? But I….Really? *Soup can?* My representative? Did you get his name? No…Well. I just…No, no, no, sir. You keep them. My payment? How much? *Really?* Huh. Alright, You have a great day too.

(He hangs up the phone.)

Where the fuck's my shirt?

(There is a knock on the door.)

Come in.

(Frank enters.)

FRANK

Morning sunshine.

JACKSON

You're here early.

FRANK

It's 4:30, Jack.

JACKSON

Shit.

FRANK

Sleep well?

JACKSON

Where's my shirt? And why the fuck is George calling me saying I sold him 3 pieces? His favorite of which, a large fucking painting of a soup can.

FRANK

He...called you?

JACKSON

To thank me for sending my representative over to show some works for sale...which he bought at the tune of 15 grand...

FRANK

Must be a rich old bastard.

JACKSON

He is...shirt?

(Frank picks the shirt up from the floor and tosses it to Jackson.)

Thanks...

(He pulls the shirt on.)

You wouldn't know anything about all this...would you, Frank?

FRANK

Why would I?

JACKSON

Who the fuck else knows me well enough to get into my studio, and go to my fucking patron…and get the exact amount that the object of my desire needs to save her gallery? Odds not in your favor, Frankie. So fucking spill.

FRANK

I…couldn't tell you, Jack.

JACKSON

Well, I…couldn't believe you, Frank. Come on at least have the respect to fucking stand up and tell me. Who fucking stole my paintings, Frank?

FRANK

I'm sorry, Jack.

JACKSON

You should be.

Frank

Jack…

JACKSON

Get out…I have a fucking headache.

FRANK

Just…

JACKSON

No! At least…not until you tell me.

FRANK

I wish I could.

JACKSON

Well, What's stopping you, Frank?

FRANK

Fear.

JACKSON

Of what? Me? *Fuck* that! Frank, as long as I've known you…I never thought I'd have to watch my back with you…

FRANK

Look: Please just trust that I had to.

JACKSON

It's hard to *trust* with a knife wound in your back…

FRANK

Is that Shakespeare?

JACKSON

Not time for fucking jokes, Frank!

FRANK

Sorry…I know it looks bad…but

JACKSON

It doesn't just *look* bad. It *is* bad.

FRANK

Snapping.

Damnit, Jackson! I had to!

JACKSON

I don't think you ever *have* to fuck over your friends.

FRANK

You don't think I had my reasons?

JACKSON

No, you had reasons. They just weren't good enough.

FRANK

How many times have I had to trust you? Now that I'm asking you...

JACKSON

Are you fucking serious?

FRANK

Oh, I understand. Once again, Jackson's being unreasonable.

JACKSON

That what you think I am, Frank?

FRANK

I didn't mean...

JACKSON

No. Tell me, Frank. Is that how you fucking see me?

FRANK

Let's just...

JACKSON

What? Forget it? No. Tell me: What am I, Frank?

FRANK

Alright! You are immature, unreasonable...and...and you're fucking blind!

JACKSON

I'm blind?

FRANK

You heard me...You're...

JACKSON

Say it, Frank. I'm *what*…

FRANK

I'm not doing this…

JACKSON

Too late, I already heard you.

FRANK

You've *never* fucking heard me!

JACKSON

Well, here's your chance. Let's hear it.

FRANK

You're…You are so busy chasing after these fucking dreams that just aren't possible. God damnit, you've been out of school two fucking years…And what do you have to show for it? That sofa? The sofa from you fucking dorm. Showing paintings that haven't evolved since undergrad…Chasing after…Chasing after a woman who has been ignoring you very successfully for years. Running away from mom and dad because they don't like what you've become…Claiming you're not giving in? That you're not selling out? That's a fucking excuse…You are just too busy running that you've yet to stop and see the terrible hell-hole that is your life…Look around you Jackson. An artist? I don't see an artist…I see a child who's yet to grow up and become an artist…An artist recognizes when something is failing and can change it. That's the principle of design, Jack…If the audience isn't there…you have to change it…That's what's wrong here. You are so busy telling everyone in your life how wrong they are that you can't even see that you are floundering…And that there are people…right here who have been trying to hold you up, but they just can't take the weight anymore and they…God damnit…they know they are loosing ground … but they would rather drown themselves than watch you fall…because they know you can be something great…But you just aren't doing it. For whatever reason…you just…aren't doing it…and I…can't hold you up anymore…

(Frank begins to exit, just as he does so, Monica enters accompanied by Martin.)

MONICA

Peacock, you'll never believe what just happened!

JACKSON

(Jackson smiles weakly.)

What?

MONICA

I'm going to buy my gallery!

JACKSON

Mon'!

(He jumps up taking her in his arms.)

I'm so happy for you.

MONICA

Martin wrote me a check!

MARTIN

Don't mention it, Babe.

JACKSON

Babe?

MONICA

Isn't that amazing, Jackson?

JACKSON

It sure is something…

MONICA

Excuse me. Can I use the restroom? I've been so excited I keep forgetting to stop by the damn restroom.

JACKSON

(Weakly laughing.)

Sure…

MARTIN

How…

(*Jackson Punches Martin.*)

JACKSON

Now Martin, no need to bleed on my floor…

(*Monica reenters, seeing Martin, she rushes to his side.*)

MONICA

What did you do?

JACKSON

He doesn't fucking deserve you!

FRANK

Jack…

MONICA

What?

JACKSON

Monica…I…damnit this guy's a prick…You…you should be with me…I'd…

MONICA

Being jealous is one thing, Jackson. But this is low even for you. Be happy for me. Be happy I didn't wind up dating a…selfish, rude…You…You're supposed to be happy for me!

JACKSON

I'm so happy, Mon'…it's just…I might not be perfect, but I know…Shit, I have to believe I'm better than…

(*He gestures to Martin.*)

That.

MONICA

It's my job to decide that.

JACKSON

How can I change your mind?

MONICA

You can't. Sweet heart…I just don't see us going very far…

JACKSON

Then I'll show you us going far…

MARTIN

Well, unfortunately for you, It's the lady's choice.

JACKSON

(Nearly to tears.)

Fine. You win, Martin.

(To Monica.)

I'll be here when you start seeing through this guy, Mon'.

MONICA

Don't…

FRANK

(A pause, Frank finally speaks, coldly.)

So…Where'd you get the money, Martin?

(Martin gapes a bit at Frank, before covering.)

MARTIN

Savings…You know that, Frank.

FRANK

Savings, right. No need to be so defensive, Martin…

(Jackson looks confusedly at Frank, then to Martin. The room is silent until Jackson speaks.)

JACKSON

You're right, Martin. Fuck, those words tasted bad. But…you're right. It's her choice. Monica…It's your fucking choice…

MONICA

(Sarcastically.)

Admirable, Jackson.

JACKSON

(Finally breaking down, allowing himself to cry.)

Shit!

(Gradually becoming more shaken.)

I never thought I'd see the day. I don't trust, Frank…And I see that you…you Monica are just like all the other women out there. Blind. Blind to a good guy…Looks like the trinity is breaking up.

MONICA

Jackson…

JACKSON

Hey, Don't worry about it, Monica. You've got your man. Be happy.

MARTIN

She will be.

JACKSON

Wonderful. Fucking wonderful! You're all happy. Let's shoot for perfect score: You know what would make my fucking night?

FRANK

What's that?

JACKSON

Seeing you all the fuck out.

FRANK

Jack, you don't know the whole story...

JACKSON

I know enough. Get out.

MARTIN

I'd love to. *We* have reservations...

FRANK

We'll talk later?

JACKSON

When I know *why*, Frank.

FRANK

I can't tell you that.

JACKSON

Then we won't be talking.

(Jackson exits into his bedroom, leaving Frank alone.)

SCENE TEN

(Lights come up on Frank's apartment, Martin is putting on his coat and Frank sits reading.)

FRANK

You're leaving?

MARTIN

Going out...

FRANK

Where?

MARTIN

I don't know. Bar, club…Why the fuck do you care?

FRANK

I just…

MARTIN

You want to come? Don't you have a knitting circle or something?

FRANK

With who, Martin?

MARTIN

Don't you-

FRANK

If you hadn't noticed, Jackson and I aren't really speaking anymore.

MARTIN

Who's fault is that?

FRANK

Yours.

MARTIN

Oh fuck off. Get your coat…I'll drop you off at a queer club…

FRANK

Martin, Do you honestly-

MARTIN

I don't know, Frank! Alright? I don't get you!

FRANK

No shit!

MARTIN

In case you hadn't noticed, Frank. No one really gets you.

FRANK

What the fuck is that supposed to mean?

MARTIN

Your *best friend?* Your best friend has no fucking clue that for 12 years you've wanted to bend him over his easel…and…you know the rest. For people to get you…You have to fucking decide who you are.

FRANK

I know who I am.

MARTIN

Maybe you should stop keeping it such a fucking secret, Frank.

FRANK

Why Martin? Who the fuck wants to know?

MARTIN

(Laughing.)

You're right, Frank. I'm leaving…

FRANK

Stay gone.

MARTIN

Take a page out of *your* fucking book.

FRANK

What are-

MARTIN

Isn't that what you did, Frank?

FRANK

What's your point?

MARTIN

He just wanted you to-

FRANK

Be someone different?

MARTIN

To be a fucking man and take the job he offered you.

FRANK

I didn't want it!

MARTIN

I did!

FRANK

You have it!

MARTIN

I was second!

(A pause.)

FRANK

Who fucking cares? You have what you want...

MARTIN

(Chuckles.)

Want...Do you *want* to teach?

FRANK

No.

MARTIN

What do you want?

FRANK

I want a life outside the Burnem family circus, Martin.

MARTIN

Earth to Frank: You have it. You just don't do anything with it.

FRANK

Are you doing what you want, Martin?

MARTIN

No one does what they want, Frank.

FRANK

Jackson does.

MARTIN

Right…*Jackson.*

FRANK

Honestly, what is your problem? I know, believe me I know, he can be off putting, but he's never done anything to you…

MARTIN

You really believe yourself don't you?

FRANK

I do.

MARTIN

He's me, Frank!

FRANK

What?

MARTIN

Until you went off to you ran off to be an artist, we were close…

FRANK

Of course we were. We were kids…The only argument there was who got to be the blue ninja turtle.

MARTIN

No, being kids had nothing to do with it.

FRANK

What was it then?

MARTIN

Your graduation. Me and Dad waited up for you until two AM…

FRANK

…What does this have to-

MARTIN

Went all out, Frank. Fucking banners and balloons…

FRANK

Martin…I didn't know.

MARTIN

It was a fucking surprise party, dip-shit, you weren't supposed to know.

FRANK

Well, If I didn't know you can't hardly blame…

MARTIN

I don't blame you. I blame Jackson.

FRANK

How-

MARTIN

After the ceremony, you marched over to your family, Mom's crying…her little baby is leaving the nest, Dad's babbling to some other dad about all these places you're going…I'm sitting there being treated like some kind of fucking trained ape, smiling and nodding, being happy for my brother…and you…march up and say…

FRANK

Oh, Christ…'I'm leaving…'

MARTIN

'…with Jack.' And walked away. Whatever hold he has on you…

(Both are silent for a moment.)

FRANK

I love him.

MARTIN

I know.

(There is an uncomfortable silence.)

FRANK

Alright, Martin…I'm not perfect. Okay?

MARTIN

No. It's not 'okay,' Frank. Don't you get that your family isn't us anymore…It's that fucking bum…

FRANK

He's not a bum.

MARTIN

Right…He's your brother.

FRANK

You're my…

(*Frank sighs.*)

You were leaving.

MARTIN

Yea…

FRANK

Bye.

MARTIN

I'll come back…

FRANK

Stay out till *two* if you want. I'm not waiting up.

(*Martin exits. Frank watches the door for a moment, then takes his coat and exit. Lights fade out on area.*)

SCENE ELEVEN

(*Lights go down on area, when they return we see Jackson in his flat, face first into a pillow. By his head there is a stereo loudly playing 'She Fucking Hates Me' by Puddle of Mudd. There is a knock on the door.*)

JACKSON

Ready to explain yourself?

FRANK

Yes, actually…

JACKSON

(*Turning down his music.*)

Well?

FRANK

Can I come in, first?

JACKSON

Talk from where you are.

FRANK

This is ridiculous...

JACKSON

Meet my demands, or talk not...

(Frank laughs.)

Don't mock me.

FRANK

Sorry, you sounded like some kind of gate keeper...Can I please come in?

JACKSON

No.

FRANK

I'm coming in.

JACKSON

Right, Frank...Break down the door...

(A loud thud, then Frank falls into the room.)

Fine...Come in.

(Looking Frank over.)

Frank.

FRANK

Jackson.

(A pause. Frank bursts out laughing.)

What is this?

(Motioning to the stereo.)

JACKSON

(Lying back on the couch face down.)

Monica and mine's song…

FRANK

Turn it off.

JACKSON

No.

FRANK

(Leaning over Jackson, turning off the music.)

There.

(Without a word, Jackson reaches up, turning it back on.)

Stop it.

(Turning the music off a second time.)

Stop wallowing in bad music long enough to listen.

(Jackson again wordlessly, turns the stereo back on.)

FRANK

Alright.

(Frank leans over Jackson, unplugs the stereo, walks with it over to the door, opens the door and drops it out.)

Ready to listen?

JACKSON

Still into his pillow.

Continue.

FRANK

Jack…The reason this happened…Would you look at me?

(Jackson sits up and meets Frank's eyes.)

JACKSON

Better?

FRANK

Yes. Jack, I…have…I'm…

JACKSON

What you are is *boring* me…

(Beginning to lean into the pillow again.)

FRANK

Jackson, I like you! I have feelings for you…I'm…I…I'm…

JACKSON

Oh, Christ. You're coming out, aren't you?

FRANK

Surprise…

(A pause. Jackson's eyes light up, showing that he now understands the situation.)

JACKSON

Holy fucking Fuck. Frank. You *like* me.

FRANK

(Nervously.)

Yea…

JACKSON

You *like* like me?

FRANK

Well, I wasn't planning on writing you a circle 'yes' or 'no' note...but in all practical purposes...You could call it that...

JACKSON

Mushy feelings?

FRANK

Yes...

JACKSON

How long?

FRANK

A while.

JACKSON

How long exactly?

FRANK

(Frustrated.)

About a week after I met you. 12 years...That's why your paintings are gone...

JACKSON

Okay...Frank...I'm not sure I follow.

FRANK

Martin was going to tell you about my...feelings...

JACKSON

The mushy ones...

FRANK

Yes...those feelings. Martin was going to tell you if I didn't agree to let him sell your paintings for the money...

JACKSON

For…Monica's gallery. That fuck…

FRANK

The night we, well, *you* got so drunk was the night…I had agreed to help Martin. He took your keys…

(*A pause.*)

JACKSON

So, he could get my paintings…And sell them to get the money for…

FRANK

Mon's gallery…I'm…sorry.

JACKSON

And now she's out to dinner with that prick…

FRANK

I'm so sorry.

JACKSON

(*After a pause.*)

Why didn't you just let him tell me, Frank?

FRANK

I didn't want things to be…awkward.

JACKSON

(*Laughing.*)

Frank…That's so…ridiculous. You completely fucked me over to avoid *awkward?*

FRANK

You aren't angry?

JACKSON

No, I'm incredibly pissed off, but…Shit.

(*Jackson smiles and chuckles.*)

So…you really have a thing for me?

FRANK

Must you…

JACKSON

Damn…That makes a lot a sense…

FRANK

What is that supposed to mean?

JACKSON

Sometimes I think you are *too* good of a friend…that just explains it.

FRANK

Jack…I'm…Sorry…

JACKSON

I know you're sorry, Frank…And, I'm sorry too.

FRANK

Why are you sorry?

JACKSON

(*Being ever full of himself, he comes off oddly flirtatious.*)

It just must have been hard…keeping those feelings to yourself…this whole time…

FRANK

(*Pathetically falling into Jackson's unintentional trap.*)

It…was terrible. What's worse is you've known for the past five minutes…and haven't reacted…

JACKSON

I've been stalling…I'm trying to process…

FRANK

I've been trying to not…to react…

JACKSON

Not to react? Oh…oh! Right. I just…Well…huh…*Well*…

(Frank leans in quickly kissing Jackson, taking him completely off guard. Just as he does so, Monica walks in.)

MONICA

(Shocked.)

You turned him.

JACKSON

(Jumping, Knocking Frank to the floor.)

Monica! There was no copulation just conversation!

MONICA

(Holding back laughter, she smiles to Frank.)

And you were choking, right?

JACKSON

I….

(Smiling.)

You came back.

MONICA

For my bag…

(She picks up her bag.)

JACKSON

Monica…

(Monica begins to exit.)

MONICA

Don't Peacock.

(Monica starts to leave again.)

FRANK

Monica!

MONICA

Frank…What?

FRANK

Monica. You are staying right fucking here.

JACKSON

Frank…

FRANK

No! You are listening to me now. Martin didn't get that money from his savings…

MONICA

What does it matter, Frank?

FRANK

Monica…That's Jackson's money.

JACKSON

Frank…

FRANK

Monica, Listen:

(Martin enters.)

MARTIN

Monica? Oh, this loser's holding you up, huh?

JACKSON

No, I want her to fucking go…

MONICA

Great. I was just leaving…

JACKSON

Good.

FRANK

(To Martin, forcefully.)

Tell her the God-damned truth.

MARTIN

What are you talking about, Frank?

FRANK

Shit, I don't know…Why don't you tell her all about how you blackmailed me into stealing Jackson's paintings so you could turn out that check that Monica here has in her bag?

MONICA

What?

MARTIN

(Laughing.)

Do you believe that? So jealous, he's got poor Frank lying to you…

JACKSON

(Softly.)

Monica…It's us. It's me. Why would I hurt you?

MONICA

You…You wouldn't.

98

MARTIN

You're going to believe this, loser?

MONICA

Completely.

JACKSON

(He smiles.)

Monica…

MONICA

Martin. I think I will have to decline that date.

MARTIN

Fuck…

MONICA

Eloquent.

MARTIN

You know what? I don't even care. See my face. You aren't that special.

JACKSON

She is and you know it.

MONICA

Aw…

JACKSON

(To Frank.)

That was good, no?

FRANK

Yea…yea, It was.

(*Sighing.*)

This is where you see yourself out Martin.

MARTIN

Fuck you…

JACKSON

(*Pushing him out the door.*)

Thanks for coming, Marty. It was a real pleasure seeing you again, We'll have to do it again sometime…blah, blah, blah…Get the fuck out of my apartment.

FRANK

(*Slamming the door.*)

Ladies and Gentlemen: My brother.

JACKSON

I can't believe you two came from the same womb.

FRANK

I try to forget it.

JACKSON

So, I guess you and Martin aren't…

MONICA

Doesn't look like it.

(*Taking the check from her bag.*)

I guess this belongs to you.

JACKSON

(*Taking the check.*)

This isn't mine. Here.

(He returns the check.)

MONICA

You're really? After I-

JACKSON

I'm working on this knight in shining armor thing...

MONICA

Jackson?

JACKSON

What?

MONICA

Shut up. For once...

(She kisses him on the cheek.)

JACKSON

Uh, Frank...

FRANK

Need a minute?

JACKSON

Hour...

(Frank begins to leave; Monica looks torn, then speaks.)

MONICA

Frank...

FRANK

I know.

MONICA

You-

FRANK

I'm fine.

JACKSON

Hey…I didn't-

FRANK

I know.

(Bowing to Jackson, smiling.)

Good morrow, Sir knight.

JACKSON

(Returning Frank's bow.)

Squire…

MONICA

You know…For this…whatever this is…to work, you and Frank are going to have to start letting me in on these little jokes.

JACKSON

I don't think it's going to work then…

(Frank exits. Monica and Jackson share a kiss. Lights fade to black. When they return Frank and Jackson address the audience for a last time.)

JACKSON

It's a little to do with sacrifice…

FRANK

Giving.

JACKSON

Laughter.

FRANK

Tears.

JACKSON

Comrades…

FRANK

Enemies…

JACKSON

Pushing…

FRANK

Pulling…

JACKSON

Acceptance…

FRANK

Admittance.

JACKSON

Realization…

FRANK

Complete oblivion…

JACKSON

Change…

FRANK

Being flat-out stubborn.

JACKSON

Trash.

FRANK

Treasure…

JACKSON

In life…

FRANK

In death…

JACKSON

The final…

FRANK

The always continuous…

JACKSON/FRANK

Art.

PART II

Portraits

Portraits, the second in this series, was written in 2014. The play, like the premieres, takes place 7 years into the lives of the characters. *Portraits* premiered at the 10th Anniversary 2014 Indy Fringe Festival at Theatre on the Square (stage two) with a new cast:

- Jackson Bell played by Taylor Cox

- Frank Burnem played by Adam Tran

- Monica Graham played by Sarah Hoback

- Scott Miller played by Anthony Logan Nathan

This play is dedicated to Taylor, Adam, Sarah, and Anthony for giving back life I didn't know was missing and for bringing back sparks. You have forever added yourselves among the threads of the canvas.

- Jackson Bell: Established and crass artist, mid to late-30s.

- Frank Burnem: A struggling art professor, mid to late-30s.

- Monica Graham-Bell: Jackson's wife, early to mid-30s, a successful gallery manager.

- Scott Miller: Also known as "coffee-refill guy", dating Frank, 40s-50s.

The play takes place 7 years after the original 'Gallery,' in the apartment lofts of Frank Burnem and and Jackson Bell.

(Two spots up on opposite stage areas. Only showing the ghostly figures of two men who speak faster and faster as the following list grows.)

JACKSON

Art.

FRANK

Art.

JACKSON

Free expression....

FRANK

My prison.

JACKSON

My former flame.

FRANK

My forever downfall.

JACKSON

What I do...

FRANK

What *I* do...

JACKSON

What buys my suits…

FRANK

What left me behind.

JACKSON

It pays the bills…

FRANK

Sometimes.

JACKSON

How I grew up.

FRANK

How I've lost my youth.

JACKSON

The feeling that you've made it…

FRANK

Or lost it.

JACKSON

Or…

FRANK

…That you never really had it.

JACKSON

The backbone of my relationships.

FRANK

What's pushed all mine away.

JACKSON

Where I both found…

FRANK

…and lost…

JACKSON

…myself…

FRANK

My drug.

JACKSON

My food.

FRANK

My retreat.

JACKSON

I retreat.

FRANK

I can't stop now…

JACKSON

I need it.

FRANK

I can't sleep.

JACKSON

It's who I am.

FRANK

It defines me.

JACKSON

I can't go back now.

FRANK

What do the neighbors think?

JACKSON

I can't show this to mom…

JACKSON/FRANK

Art.

(In blackout, three knocks on a door and then the turning of the knob are heard. Lights up, Frank Burnem, sits in reading glasses and robe reading a book. He glances at the turning knob and rolls his eyes.)

JACKSON

(off stage.)

You aren't fucking some beefy, shaved guy with a huge cock are you?

FRANK

You'd come in even if I said, yes, I don't quite understand this evening's formality…

JACKSON

(entering.)

If you don't want me here regularly, then why, prey-tell do I have a key? Let's face it; you give keys to boyfriends, girlfriends, or common-law-married-straight-best-friends, because you *want* to, rather, you *need* to, see them every day.

FRANK

I live in staggering fear that one day I will have gone so long without seeing you, that I will not be able to paint your visage from memory and that will be the day I will end it, Jack.

JACKSON

(sitting)

We both know you're resolved to painting bowls of fruit and sad still-lives. Portraits are beyond you.

FRANK

Welcome home.

JACKSON

I might just be here to visit, Frank. Don't you fucking welcome me to your sofa, just yet...

FRANK

Well, if you aren't staying, I'm calling Scott.

JACKSON

Do *not* give 'coffee refill guy ' a name, Frank. You fuck coffee refill guy *that*, is what you've become.

FRANK

You've become married. I'm assuming you're not fucking anything but your left hand.

JACKSON

Right hand.

FRANK

Of course. You're right handed, more dexterous, I suppose.

JACKSON

I'm ambidextrous. I just like the familiar touch of my dominant hand. Why do I continue to share my glowing radiance with you?

FRANK

You're addicted, we're both addicted to the pain. My therapist says I'm my own worst enemy.

JACKSON

You can't afford a therapist.

FRANK

It's an app...

JACKSON

She kicked me out.

FRANK

Well, at least it wasn't out of the closet, like she did me…

JACKSON

Every girl you *didn't* fuck in college did that, don't you go blaming Monica.

FRANK

What did you do?

JACKSON

I fucked up an ugly sofa with some red paint. I honestly think it looks better now than it did.

FRANK

You two have always have had differing tastes…

JACKSON

…In the same medium, Frank. *Always*, in the same medium. I used to love our arguments about art. I did, it's why I fell in love…

FRANK

I know. You argued yourself to the alter, perhaps not the best induction into married life, but who am I to throw stones?

JACKSON

You really shouldn't be tossing anything my direction from your glass house of depressing celibacy.

FRANK

To what do I owe the unsurprising honor?

(Picking his book back up to continue reading.)

JACKSON

I think I'm unlovable, Frank, I really do. She's a god-damned goddess and I can't even *not* ruin her new sofa. I'm a bull in a china shop, she picked me up and turned me into something real and now I can't live up to her vision. I think, I'm her biggest regret, as an artist.

(Frank sighs and closes the book.)

FRANK

You've been together since middle school.

JACKSON

No, that's the fucking thing, isn't it, Frank? I pined after her since middle school, I've only, as you said, been together, for 7 years…It takes 'being together' to get how someone who used to *glow* from across the lunch room could look like Dr. Evil's bald cat in the morning…that's what you get with 7 years 'together', Frank….bald fucking cats…

FRANK

Want a beer?

JACKSON

What do you have?

FRANK

Stella and a few Rolling Rocks…

JACKSON

Wonderful, the cheap shit, not too cheap, but cheap. I'll take a Stella, it's been a while.

FRANK

(Retrieving 2 beers.)

Grossly, complains the successful artist. One day some crass undergraduate can write a scathing paper on your tragic lack of technique or claim you're the savoir of modern art, one of the two.

(He hands Jackson a beer.)

JACKSON

I am giving a guest lecture next week…

FRANK

You are not. Where?

JACKSON

It's not important…

FRANK

Jackson.

JACKSON

Parsons.

FRANK

The school of art and design?

JACKSON

The same, mon ami.

(The two toast, clicking their glasses.)

FRANK

Shit. I can't even get Parsons to take my calls.

JACKSON

Don't read into it, Frank. You have pieces in museums. I'm going to have to die before I have pieces anywhere but my living room.

FRANK

Museum.

JACKSON

(Drinking.)

What?

FRANK

I have *a* piece in *a* museum. You said museums, it's one piece...one museum.

JACKSON

Don't be so modest, it's disgusting. Want to play the guest? Be my muse? My mentor?

FRANK

Of course not. It's your turn to spread your wings and die behind the podium. Teaching! Congratulations, my friend, you have made it.

JACKSON

How do you do it, Frankie?

FRANK

I died inside a long time ago, only when the artist dies can he speak freely on art history without all these problematic opinions. You're still rotting, just die already and teach.

JACKSON

You're an awful muse.

FRANK

(He stands and exits into his bedroom, yelling back to Jackson from there.)

It's not my fault that you chose poorly. Most straight modernists pick a beautiful girl, or a celebrity; you picked your depressing queer friend. I think this is more on you, than me.

JACKSON

I think my marriage is over, Frank.

FRANK

I know you do.

JACKSON

(lighting a cigarette.)

So, what's new with you?

(Frank re-enters dressed, no longer in his robe.)

FRANK

You smoke now?

JACKSON

I want to age into more of a Warhol, in a cloud of smoke and mystery; I might start wearing turtle necks.

FRANK

Don't. It will make your face look fat. You hate Warhol.

JACKSON

He's grown on me. Make my face look fat? How gay are you?

FRANK

As gay, as you would look costumed in a turtle neck.

JACKSON

Want to order a pizza?

(Frank takes the cigarette from Jackson and puts it out into a mug, then takes his spot back on the sofa.)

FRANK

Only the greasy place delivers this late. I hate the greasy place…

JACKSON

Who cares? I'm buying.

FRANK

We're both getting fat.

JACKSON

We're getting old. Fuck, we *are* old, we're fat, we're alone, get me the number to the greasy place, it is surely our last recourse.

(Frank removes a cellphone from his pocket, makes some swipes and hands it to Jackson. Lights fade on area. A sudden bright spot flashes on; perhaps with a sound effect in tandem bringing to mind the feeling of a confessional style lit room. Frank, as if by necessity, addresses the audience.)

116

FRANK

Art school in New York was absolutely the farthest place my parents should have sent me if they wanted my attentions to fall on any of the nice *girls*, with whom, mom was perpetually attempting to set me up. Until school, I had been winning my game of hide and seek with an expert power-play of denial and residency in the closet. I limited my passions to my portfolio and purposely left myself no time for friends or fornication. I kept a strict regimen of studious solitude that was not shaken until I quite literally got the wind knocked out of me, twice.

(Sitting.)

I am crippled with the same, vivid reoccurring day-dream. If I let my mind wonder, I always find myself on the ground, heaving for air and franticly patting the grass around me in search of my glasses. This day, the day I lost my air, is a memory completely untouched by the tarnish of age. I found myself and the sketches I carried with me, suddenly, on the ground. It would seem that my classmate didn't quite agree with my rather scathing critique of his latest artistic abortion and wished to offer his rebuttal. So, he threw me to the ground and rebuttaled his foot right into my stomach, repeatedly. As I drew the breath I conceited to be my last, a glorious shadow appeared. In a single punch, my tormentor's nose began spewing the most satisfying shade of Goya-esque red I've ever seen. In this brief, bloody reprieve, I was able to locate my glasses, and get a proper view of my savoir. A paint covered, scruffy, and shocked freshmen stood over myself and my attacker, holding his hand. He quickly helped me gather my sketches and then mouthed the words "I think we should run." In my haze, I foolishly ended his escape plan by asking, "Why?" As the clumsy word left my lips, I was once again caught in a blizzard of sketches and was met on the ground my unkempt defender, who somehow managed to land nearly exclusively on my testicles, leaving me again, without air. "Because I can't fight for shit…" He admitted. Our now mutual enemy, satisfied with ending us both horizontal on the grass, exited into the now setting sun, dribbling that beautiful shade of Goya red along the grass as he went. Then silence. Silence only finally cut with, "Are you okay?" No. I wasn't 'okay.' I wasn't *okay* at all. I was in love. Instantly and unapologetically with a dirty and clearly straight freshmen, whom I later learned was failing every class. My first memory of Jackson, blurry, lucky and cocky, remains among a mental scrapbook running years long, in crystal-clear high definition.

(A pause.)

I'm forever, figuratively picking popcorn kernels from the teeth of my emotionally dense, socially flawed friends. It's just that I can't seem to catch a glimpse of my own form. Now, with age, I find my arm sore from years of holding a hand mirror to Jackson Bell's furiously soiled reflection. Since that day, I have found my glasses, but I realize I have spent most of my adult life, patting the grass, trying to find ways I can save *him*. Be it from himself, poverty, critique, or battles with house hold appliances he never learned to operate, I've paid my dues for his single, lucky punch, because true love, requited or no, is endless and constant and changing. I have built my personal prison with bricks resembling every one of Jackson's failures, tirelessly, holding a mirror, spending my entire artistic career trying to mix an honest of shade of blood red...and my entire life trying to lift the mirror to myself.

(Lights suddenly out, in the same way they came up.)

SCENE TWO

(Lights up on Monica and Jackson eating TV dinners at home, both wearing formal wear.)

MONICA

(looking into the dinner box.)

What's the grey?

JACKSON

I think it's pudding. Or potatoes.

(Scooping a bite from his plate, feeding it to her.)

You tell me.

(She bats his hand away.)

MONICA

Stop it. Your nails are gross.

JACKSON

I can't believe you were kissing Kroachivelli's ass...

MONICA

He's the best-selling, headlining gallery name; I would have sucked his dick if he asked.

JACKSON

I can do another show.

MONICA

I am not sucking your dick. And you have your lecture. Are you ready? Did you talk to Frank about it?

JACKSON

Figured I'd wing it.

MONICA

Frank said no?

JACKSON

Didn't really come up.

MONICA

Fine, Dear, you wing your lecture and I'll beg archaic Pols to put something, anything on my vacant gallery walls.

JACKSON

I just said I'd do a show.

MONICA

Well, I'm not sucking your dick.

(After a pause.)

JACKSON

Jackson me off, then?

MONICA

No. Stop. Stop that, stop saying 'Jackson off,' it's not cute, it's not funny it only garishly shows of your frightening narcissism.

JACKSON

Frank thinks it's hilarious…

MONICA

…No he doesn't…

JACKSON

…Whatever. That's great wifey, dearest, go suck Kroachivelli's dick, I am sure that paintings of humanoid animals will not be a fading fad. No egg or…ah…other white materials on my darling's face, I won't have it.

(He goes in for a kiss, she pushes him back)

MONICA

Oh, shut up. You were flirting with Gerty. I saw it. She's like 85, Jackson.

JACKSON

Flirting sure, but I am not performing any oral. What's wrong with you, should I wash my hands?

MONICA

I hate art. And it's years of decay, Jackson, washing your hands isn't getting me anymore in the mood.

JACKSON

Fine. You hate art? Come on, don't we all? It's all politics and sucking old Polish testicles, like Kroachivelli's.

(Monica silently picks at her plate.)

Look at us, we're sitting here in gallery formal, eating freeze-dried macaroni. Baby, We are art.

MONICA

(Still picking at the food)

Sure, in…depressing grey scale, please tell me what that is?

JACKSON

I love you.

MONICA

No, you love…

JACKSON/MONICA

…a good composition.

JACKSON

Why do you always, say that?

MONICA

It's just a silly little thing, Peacock.

JACKSON

You haven't called me Peacock in years.

MONICA

I think Kroachivelli got me drunk.

JACKSON

I knew I was getting laid.

MONICA

What's the point of it, Jackson?

JACKSON

Sex?

MONICA

Art. Why do we do it?

JACKSON

Because I love it.

(A pause.)

Right?

MONICA

I guess you must. Let's paint something together.

JACKSON

Now? I'm tired, Mon'…

MONICA

Oh. my God, Jackson. You are my father.

JACKSON

Don't you try your David Mamet shit on me, I'm just tired. I don't think you are fat, I am not leaving you and I am not cheating. I am tired. I am drunk. And I don't want to paint. After spending all night in a gallery with a group of dick sucking, titty-fucking, one-upping artists…I don't think I will ever paint again.

MONICA

Just sofas, then?

JACKSON

Frank got let go.

MONICA

God, again?

JACKSON

I know.

MONICA

You should do something.

JACKSON

That's why I was hitting on Gerty. I was trying to get him on at the college she donates to. Fuck, If Frank Burnem can't get work, where are we going?

MONICA

Infomercials. Frank's getting fat. You think he's depressed?

JACKSON

Frank looks better with some meat one his bones.

MONICA

Is he still talking to…

JACKSON

…coffee refill guy…

MONICA

…Scott.

JACKSON

I think so. I don't think he's head over heels, but they are talking and fucking. Talking and fucking, the American dream…

MONICA

That's good.

(Jackson begins clearing the dishes.)

JACKSON

Who called before?

MONICA

My dad.

JACKSON

What did Old Man Graham want today?

MONICA

He thinks you're stuck

JACKSON

Are you fucking kidding me, Monica?

MONICA

I told him you were getting work. He said that you might not be out of work, but you are very much stuck. He says you are making sales, not art. I think he wanted to help you.

JACKSON

With what? I sell something, *daily*, you're wearing, who?

MONICA

…Dior.

JACKSON

…And, we're drinking 25-year old aged wine with these T.V. dinners.

MONICA

That's not what he means, that's not what I mean.

JACKSON

You want me to take a retreat into the woods? Become a drunk?

MONICA

(under her breath.)

You're already drunk…

JACKSON

…Become Pollock? Is that what you guys want? You want me to come back making spin-art or finger paints, claiming that I, after 20 years, have finally found my raw, visceral and uninhibited self in splatter art? Is that what you want?

MONICA

I just want you to be happy…The old Jackson…

JACKSON

You and Frank are both lusting after this old Jackson, yet here sits Jackson, old. I'm right here. Sorry I've let my ass go to shit…

MONICA

Your ass looks fine. Your paintings look fine. And that's just the thing Jackson…everything is fine. But is *fine* really your goal?

JACKSON

I'm burning my suits.

MONICA

You're drunk. It has nothing to do with the suits. It has everything to do with what's inside the suits.

(Jackson makes a disgusted face and mimes vomiting.)

JACKSON

(mocking her.)

It's what's inside the suits? *You're* fucking drunk, *I'm* burning the suits. The old Jackson, who clearly has a better ass, would burn the suits.

(Exiting into his bedroom, returning with a blue suit.)

MONICA

Fine, none of them fit right anyway. You refuse to go to a tailor, the blue one eats you alive…the arms are way too…

JACKSON

…this one?

MONICA

(looking behind her.)

That one. Sit down. I just never thought the indomitably offensive force I married would ever be suited for *'fine.'*

JACKSON

(sitting, sadly, quoting.)

We have art in order to not die of the truth.

MONICA

Friedrich Nietzsche.

JACKSON

I think that's the point.

MONICA

Of art?

JACKSON

Yes, of art. To…not die of the truth. See? I'm not that drunk.

MONICA

You always philosophize better with a buzz.
(The two click their wine glasses in a toast. Lights fade on area.)

SCENE THREE

(Frank enters the room in pajamas and Jackson is face down on the couch in boxers, snoring as lights come up.)

FRANK

(singing.)

Good morning star shine, The Earth says 'hello.'

JACKSON

(said in yawn)

It's too early for your gay to be showing, Frank. Stop singing at me…

FRANK

Put your pants back on.

JACKSON

What was that, Sound of Music?

FRANK

Hair. Put your pants back on.

JACKSON

God Frank, don't you think I'm pretty anymore?

FRANK

You're beautiful, for all that you are and all that you will never be and put your pants on.

JACKSON

Fuck, is the Queen coming over?

FRANK

One of them, yes.

JACKSON

Scott's coming over here? I don't want to see coffee fucking refill guy not...pouring my fucking coffee, it's weird, Frank.

FRANK

My deepest apologies, Jackson, but when I made the plans for a casual lunch, I did not know I was going to be hosting sofa boarders.

(Sitting down next to him.)

What happened to you guys?

JACKSON

I don't know, Frank. I don't. Enough about me, Frank, how's your love life?

FRANK

I like him.

JACKSON

Did you tell him that?

FRANK

Of course, not. You don't just tell guys you like them.

JACKSON

I will never get you gays.

(A knock is heard at the door.)

FRANK

Put your god-damned pants on.

(Jackson reaches for his pants, and Frank opens the door, revealing Scott.)

SCOTT

Looking radiant as always.

FRANK

Please, I'm getting greys. Let me grab a coat…

(Scott enters. Jackson is still fumbling with his pants.)

Oh, you're coming in. That's wonderful…

SCOTT

Greys be damned, I always hoped to be with a distinguished artist before I die…

(Scott stops seeing Jackson fumbling with his pants.)

JACKSON

It's not like that! I'm like his wife, he doesn't even try to touch me anymore.

SCOTT

I don't think I would have ever given up.

JACKSON

You're boyfriend still thinks I'm pretty, Frank.

FRANK

Get to know him better; you'll be taking a much more hands-off approach.

SCOTT

You are so catty.

(To Jackson.)

Isn't he cute when he's catty?

JACKSON

Adorable.

SCOTT

(*Holding his hand out to Jackson.*)

Scott. I've served your coffee.

JACKSON

(*Reaching for a beer that was left on the table, taking a sip.*)

Oh, you are that guy, the coffee refill guy, I never would have guessed…

SCOTT

It's almost weird not seeing you at the diner…

JACKSON

Yeah, it's sur-fucking-real…

FRANK

Jack…

JACKSON

(*Patting the sofa next to him for Scott to sit*)

So, tell me about yourself, Scott. You pour coffee and fuck dudes, what else do you for fun?

SCOTT

(*sitting.*)

That's about all there is to it.

JACKSON

What a catch, Frank. He's got dreams.

FRANK

I know why your marriage is over, Jackson.

SCOTT

Married and straight? You must be miserable.

JACKSON

Terribly. Your boyfriend is a real class act, Frank.

FRANK

Not…

SCOTT

See, Most queens get married after the first shag, but not Frank Burnem, he'll make you wait.

JACKSON

What's your fucking problem, Frank? I'll marry the guy, fucking class act over here, Frankie. I thought you said you liked him.

FRANK

Jack, have you invested in a good life-insurance policy? I'd hate to see Monica struggle.

SCOTT

He said he liked me?

JACKSON

Right before you sashayed in.

FRANK

Jackson…

JACKSON

Which is fucking great, because I don't need him to be any more of a cat lady…

SCOTT

(To Frank.)

Wow. You said he was…funny.

(Frank chuckles.)

JACKSON

Funny? Frank's a smart man, I doubt he was that lack-luster in his description.

FRANK

Come on, Jack…

SCOTT

Just hilarious.

JACKSON

I know, I am god-damned delight. Please, come home with me and tell my wife that.

SCOTT

I'd follow you home any day. As long as you kept your mouth shut.

JACKSON

Or full?

FRANK

I'm going to hang myself. Tonight. Tonight is the night.

JACKSON

Is my ass still alright, Scott?

SCOTT

It's your best work, yet.

JACKSON

Thank you.

FRANK

I don't know what Monica ever saw in you.

JACKSON

I've got a huge dick.

(A pause.)

So, more on you, Scott. Scott, who Frank likes.

SCOTT

What do you want to know?

JACKSON

I have to know, is Frank just dynamite in the sack?

FRANK

(*Exiting into the kitchen.*)

I'm getting a beer. Or 5.

JACKSON

Get me one.

FRANK

Fuck yourself, Jackson.

JACKSON

See how he talks to me? I hope he treats you better, Scott, really I do.

SCOTT

I appreciate you developing some concern for me, because you never tip.

JACKSON

I'm a god-damned painter, Scott, the only tip I have is on my dick.

SCOTT

If you're expecting my retort there, I am not planning on humoring you with it.

JACKSON

Honest. I like that in a man.

(*Frank walks in drinking a beer.*)

SCOTT

So, tell me Jackson, what are you accomplishing with your daily performances?

JACKSON

Not a God-damned thing, Scott. Not even an Academy Award.

SCOTT

You're Vivien Leigh in Gone with the Wind. It's a damn shame the academy has withheld your nod, you play the impenetrable asshole so well.

JACKSON

Be honest with me, Scott, the only part of that that offends you is the *impenetrable* part.

SCOTT

That's all you got?

JACKSON

It's early, and if you wanted to make a gayer reference you should have gone with Elizabeth Taylor. I'm much more of a Virginia Woolf.

(Scott laughs)

SCOTT

I'm impressed, Frank. To think I thought you were exaggerating.

JACKSON

Does he say my name in bed, Scott?

SCOTT

Only once, get over yourself.

FRANK

Jesus fucking Christ…

(He goes to the kitchen again, coming back holding a second beer.)

SCOTT

Don't be so hard on him Frank, he's just a misfit toy afraid to be outgrown…

FRANK

(Opening the second beer.)

Fuck my life.

SCOTT

So, Jackson, shall we try again? You must be exhausted.

JACKSON

I have stamina.

SCOTT

I'm sure your wife would tell me differently.

JACKSON

Ask her, she needs a gal pal.

SCOTT

We will do brunch. I'll pay, because I am civil.

JACKSON

You're so perfectly civil, I'd love to shake your hand.

SCOTT

I'll reintroduce myself.

(Shaking Jackson's hand.)

I'm Scott. I'm gay. I serve your coffee. I got my degree in dance. Dance, perhaps the only art more dead and fleeting than your painting. Well, there is always the theatre…

JACKSON

Bravo, Scott, you want the passive aggressive metal? Frank and I usually wait to compete during the Olympics but you, my friend, are floating through the finish line ribbons right the fuck now.

SCOTT

I'd hate to usurp your title, but I would look great in a metal. So, tell me Jackson, why in the world would someone as educated, kind, and handsome as Frank, suffer your painfully pompous narcissism if there wasn't more to you than a stream of intelligent vulgarity?

JACKSON

Fuck me…

SCOTT

No thanks, answer my question.

(Frank exits into the kitchen again.)

FRANK

Tequila!

JACKSON

What, exactly, do you want from me, Tiny Dancer?

SCOTT

I would have settled for a pleasant meeting, but I'll take one honest answer.

(Frank pours himself a shot.)

JACKSON

I'm still a little drunk, honest it is.

(Frank takes the shot.)

I don't know. I literally live everyday wondering why people like Frank Burnem would even bat their fucking eye at me. Frank: a technical master. My wife: the smartest woman on this planet. Together these two people pulled me from the gutter of painting shock value ejaculations and rose me to this mild and pathetic success you so eloquently summed up whilst I was sleeping on my friend's sofa because I can't just apologize to my wife from ruining her new purchased…measure of success. And, because I refuse to be wrong. Some guy who fucking refills my friend's coffee in hopes of…what…are you a top or bottom Frank?

(Frank sighs, pouring another shot.)

Some guy slinging sugar packets in hopes of landing some ass, figured me out during our first real conversation outside of asking if I want fries or onion rings and all I can say is, 'I don't know.' I don't know why Frank has ever spent a second with me. But he has…since I was like 19…he just…fucking has. They both have. She can do better. Frank can do better. Shit, he did do better…

(Jackson stands, grabs his jacket and takes the shot from Frank's hand and starts to go.)

Frank you did better. He's smart, he's cute; just tell him you fucking like him. I'm going home…

(He takes Frank's beer. He exits. There is a long pause.)

SCOTT

So. Where do you want to eat?

(Frank sits.)

FRANK

I don't know.

SCOTT

Your friend's nice.

(Frank laughs.)

FRANK

I think he likes you.

SCOTT

Rumor has it you do too. Maybe you have bad taste.

FRANK

(Frank standing and picking up discarded beers and cups from the space.)

I wake up, every day, knowing that I am getting older and older, yet farther and farther away from knowing who the fuck I am.

SCOTT

Oh stop. You're young.

FRANK

A long time ago, I knew I was never going to be the painter, the artiste, because I knew that was my friend's duty, so I figured I'd teach. I did that, because that is what we are supposed to do, right?

SCOTT

Sure.

FRANK

We're supposed to grow up, we're supposed to stop dreaming and pick the next best thing. We picked, didn't we? You're expected to give up, not entirely, just a little. Get close, make a little money and die happy. That's what *we* did. Because, we do it right. We get straight A's. We get jobs. We get new sofas and designer glasses, because in this sick world, that is what is seen as right. Then, you look at someone like Jackson…

SCOTT

Oh, God, must I?

FRANK

Hear me out, someone who is immoveable. Someone who never apologizes that he won't just do the right thing and give up. Someone who without me or his wife would still be living, perhaps, squatting in, a run-down flat, below his means, because…he paints. He just does it. We can't hate him or fault him because he doesn't have it in his composition to not. He's miserable. He stopped painting. Not literally, but I hope you see what I mean. He's just holding down a job. I plucked the colors off of the peacock, because…for whatever reason that's what's right. But, at the end of the day, he might have been happier eating ramen noodles and painting away, really painting. At this point, if I left him…it just…well, it wouldn't be fair. We're artists, we're friends, the two of us are meant to be miserable, together.

(Frank is collecting more trash, but is stopped by Scott who takes a remote from Frank and sets it back on the table.)

SCOTT

Maybe so, but are you hungry or just miserable?

(Lights fade on area.)

SCENE FOUR

(Jackson sits on the sofa flipping through T.V. channels, wearing paint-covered clothes, absent-mindedly twirling a paintbrush. Monica enters with leftovers.)

JACKSON

How are the girls?

MONICA

Frank's a man dear, I've seen his penis.

JACKSON

What? When?

(Jackson switches off the T.V.)

MONICA

Besides the point, don't you think?

(She exits into the kitchen, the door of a fridge is heard.)

JACKSON

What did I do this time?

MONICA

(re-entering the room.)

I'm sure you'd be devastated to know that not every lunch shared between Frank and I centers on you. Why the fuck are you on my sofa?

JACKSON

(standing.)

I was under the impression that this model was made for sitting, my apologies.

MONICA

It's a white god-damned sofa, Jackson. A white fucking sofa that I just had cleaned and you plant your…pretentious, self-centered ass on it while you are wearing painter's clothes. Your…same…fucking…smelly painting clothes. I had to clean the fucking…sofa…because you were mixing your palate on it and now…you're just sitting…

JACKSON

Standing by…

MONICA

…sitting on my white fucking sofa in those same rancid painting clothes.

JACKSON

I didn't know I wasn't supposed to sit on the sofa.

MONICA

Yes, you did! You're a smart man, aren't you? Right? You're not an idiot? Tell me you are not a fucking idiot.

JACKSON

I'd…like to think I'm a fairly educated…

MONICA

Then why were you on my sofa!?

JACKSON

Jesus Christ, who the fuck are you!?

(He jumps on the sofa.)

All is lost, Monica, the sitting cushions may get soiled!

MONICA

Get the fuck down.

JACKSON

No!

MONICA

(She rushes to the coffee table and begins to throw magazines at him.)

Get off the sofa! Never sit on it again!

JACKSON

Am I an out-door husband now?

MONICA

Yes!

JACKSON

Well, you should fucking warn the neighbors that I will shitting outside, now!

MONICA

Get. Off. The. Sofa.

JACKSON

No, you get on the sofa! Be a normal person. Jump on the white fucking sofa with me.

MONICA

Normal people don't jump on their white sofas! Normal grown men…don't jump on their sofas.

JACKSON

Normal men fuck on their sofas!

MONICA

What?

JACKSON

If we were still normal we would have fucked on that sofa, so many times, by now!

MONICA

I knew you jerked off in here last week! The cushion was flipped!

JACKSON

Yeah. I did. I do like every Tuesday. Around 2. It's like the happiest part of my week.

(Holding his hand out to her.)

MONICA

You're an animal.

JACKSON

You knew that going in. Come here.

(Pulling her up to stand on the sofa with him.)

It feels good to be bad, doesn't it?

MONICA

There's footprints on the cushions.

JACKSON

Who gives a fuck?

(Pulling her into him, slow dancing awkwardly on the sofa.)

I'm sorry.

MONICA

No, you're not.

JACKSON

Yes. I am. I'm sorry I let you go with white.

(Monica chuckles.)

I'm sorry I'm a pain in your ass. I'm sorry my painting clothes smell.

MONICA

It's like…

(Sniffing Jackson's painting clothes)

…burnt broccoli…

JACKSON

I'm sorry you married me, you and Frank belong together. You belong together with a whole living room of white furniture and tasteful paintings, throwing cocktail parties that I would be lucky to be the drunk guest at. But, you're not Frank's type…

(She laughs.)

I'm sorry I let it come to this. I'm sorry we ever went to an IKEA. I'm sorry I ever made any real money. I'm sorry I'm miserable.

(He spins her around to face their living room.)

I'm sorry this is what matters now. It never should have. We bought that painting. We're both better painters than that, but we *bought* that. And that, I don't even know what that is…

MONICA

It's an electric tea maker. It was like three hundred dollars.

JACKSON

I've never once made tea.

MONICA

Me neither.

(He lowers his voice.)

JACKSON

What happened?

MONICA

I don't know.

JACKSON

Dance with me.

(She steps down and exits. Jackson slowly sinks onto the sofa and lights fade on area, but like before another confessional style spot quickly appears, this time, Monica addresses the audience.)

MONICA

I'm sure his transferring to my middle-school was not meant to be a malicious attack on me, but then, I hated no one more. In one week, Jackson had usurped my throne, my cling to fame, the one thing I had that wasn't ridiculously normal: Art class. Mrs. Cavanaugh, my 5th grade art teacher, would literally wait expectantly for Jackson to finish his assignment. She had abandoned me, so it became my goal to make this new boy cry. Hard. I decided I would have to plan my attack, it became an obsession, it became a bulleted list…It became a whole notebook. I still remember the image of him the day I decided to pounce. He was wearing dirty jeans, which he'd drawn on, a ratty Jem And The Holograms t-shirt; because even at 12, Jackson was always truly, truly outrageous, and he was also sporting a shiny new black eye. My plan was to present my rival with a bulleted list of the reasons I disliked him but instead, "Are you okay?" came out. Weeks of planning, and I said, "Are you okay?" And he didn't say anything. My plan never came to fruition, because the next week, Jackson was absent. And for 2 more weeks, his seat remained vacant. When he returned, the black eye had cleared, but his right arm was broken and his hand and fingers were bruised. He sat miserably, half-heartedly finger painting for the next month. After school he'd sit on a swing, not swinging, but staring into the vacant lot behind the school's playground. And one day, I guess, on June 2nd, I joined him on the swings. His arm was out of the hard cast and now in a brace that he could remove during art class. "How did you break it.?" he smiled and sarcastically replied, "*I didn't break it.*" It was the grin that doomed me and we became fast friends. We both loved the Ninja Turtles and the art of Claude Monet. He introduced me to Gustav Metzger, the music of The Cure, and he destroyed my Lisa Frank trapper keeper, on purpose. Through the years, I found myself holding onto every one of his secrets like gold. I would sneak him into my house to sleep over, innocently of course, when, for whatever reason, he didn't want to go home. Being the only one allowed in made me special enough, I didn't need art class anymore; I had an interesting and increasingly attractive shadow. On June 2nd, 15 years after we met, he asked me to marry him. June 2nd. He remembered the date of our first real conversation on the swings. That made our years in high school and college make so much more since. Things like the year he made my prom date cry by entering into a religious debate pertaining to the fact that there is no after life, became sweetly jealous and not at all malicious. When I told my father about my plans to wed my oldest friend, I could tell he wasn't happy and that he wasn't surprised. I didn't find out until the arthritis in his wrist flared up the night of our honeymoon that his father had broken his arm and hand and that Jackson was always kind of glad he did…

(Lights suddenly switch off into blackout.)

SCENE FIVE

(Jackson is sleeping face down on a sofa, Scott stands with a coffee mug in a robe watching him. Jackson wakes and cracks his neck.)

SCOTT

Hello, there.

JACKSON

(startled.)

Jesus Christ. When did you float in?

SCOTT

Last night. You were already snoring like…a little angel.

JACKSON

You two didn't fuck while I was here, please tell me you didn't fuck…

SCOTT

We didn't fuck.

JACKSON

You're just telling me that because I told you to tell me…

SCOTT

Yup.

JACKSON

Where's Frank?

SCOTT

Still asleep.

JACKSON

Wore him out, huh?

SCOTT

Maybe. What color did you paint the sofa this time?

JACKSON

Blue.

(Scott laughs and goes to exit, Jackson begins speaking, stopping him.)

It was supposed to be inspiring or beautiful. Maybe, just real?

(He makes room for Scott on the sofa, Scott sits.)

Like in those movies made by really pretentious, tiny studios, where all the titles and captions are written in papyrus and the soundtrack is done by some band only 20 year old hipsters have heard of…those fucking movies that make smart college girls cry. Movies about nothing…She was supposed to dance with me on the sofa, but she just locked herself in the study. The…fucking study that we have…what the fuck we are studying…I don't know…but she should have been dancing. Dancing with me…

SCOTT

But she didn't. Timing is everything, Jackie.

JACKSON

That it is…

(A pause.)

Jackson. Or Jack, if you are Frank. But, never 'Jackie.'

SCOTT

Fair enough. He never shuts up about you. We got fondue the other day; I witnessed a gay man talk through fondue. I think the famous greys mostly belong to you.

JACKSON

Frank worries too damned much.

SCOTT

People worry most about the ones they love.

JACKSON

Oh, that was…awful.

(A pause.)

You really give a shit about Frank, right?

SCOTT

A couple shits, yeah.

JACKSON

Good.

SCOTT

You do too, in your way.

(Frank steps into the room from his bedroom and stops in the doorway eavesdropping.)

JACKSON

Frank deserves whatever…the fuck Frank wants. Not this fucking bullshit life. Frank should have gallery shows, not me. I'm a fucking shock value hack who married the right bitch with the right father, but Frank is a god damn genius. Don't you fucking say word one of this to that fucking diva with a palate, but the way he creates shadow baffles me. It fucking baffles me, Scott. Have you seen his painting of the Chotchkies? It's a painting of fucking shit on a shelf and it means something, what, I don't know, but something, because the shadow falling from the little glass deer to the feather is so mindboggling that you don't even care that you are looking at a painting of some crap in Frank's bedroom…because that shadow *means* something. I paint something naked or gory and everyone says I'm edgy, Frank just paints and nobody says anything. No one ever says enough to Frank. No one thanks him for being more tolerant than God of sinners…but they should, Scott. They should kiss his fucking hairy feet, hairiest feet outside of a damn hobbit, am I right, Scott?

(He stops and sighs)

Someone needs to tell Frank that his fucking shadows are mindboggling. Someone needs to say something about it.

(Frank backs into the bedroom.)

SCOTT

Your stuff is better than naked gore.

JACKSON

Thank you.

SCOTT

Frank always says that you can put more life into a piece than any artist alive. He says your paintings actually breathe, that there's something about how you clearly don't give a fuck about the directional existence of light in your pieces, which makes everything you do seem so alive. Literally mobile…And he wishes he could do that…

JACKSON

He said that?

SCOTT

He never shuts up about you.

JACKSON

You know who really hates my work?

SCOTT

Most critics?

JACKSON

Don't be fucking cute, Scott. My wife.

(Scott stands to leave)

SCOTT

Good night, Jackson.

JACKSON

Just, don't fuck while I am here.

SCOTT

I wouldn't dream of it.

(A pause.)

How long are you going to be here?

JACKSON

Jesus, is Frank that fucking good in bed that you just can't wait for me to leave?

SCOTT

Go to bed, Jackie, it's early.

JACKSON

What the fuck time is it?

SCOTT

5 AM. I was just getting something to wet the whistle. Good night, Jackson.

JACKSON

Aw, fuck, you two just did it, didn't you?

SCOTT

Good night, Jackson.

(Scott exits, Jackson lies back down and the lights fade on area.)

SCENE SIX

(Lights up on Scott and Frank seated on the sofa, Jackson on the floor, all three paying extremely close attention to the television.)

JACKSON

3...2...1...dead cat! I called it, dead cat, you owe me a beer.

(Scott sighs and pushes himself off the sofa, going to the kitchen and retrieving Jackson a beer.)

FRANK

How do you not smell that?

JACKSON

This is Hoarders, Frank not Clean House, I'm sure there are worse smells than petrified pussy.

(Scott hands Jackson the beer and sits back down.)

SCOTT

We could ask your wife...

(Jackson half-heartily punches Scott.)

ROACHES! Drink!

(Jackson opens the beer and clicks glasses with Frank, both of them take drinks.)

JACKSON

You are learning well the ways of Sunday afternoon Hoarders sessions. I salute you.

SCOTT

You two do this often?

FRANK

Every Sunday since Jackson added to Monica's last piece.

JACKSON

It needed…

FRANK

It absolutely didn't need a fuchsia and teal cock, Jackson. Absolutely not.

JACKSON

It fucking needed something…

FRANK

Well, now it has a phallic focal point…

SCOTT

And tears…there's the tears…

JACKSON

(mockingly.)

Take my dignity but not my trash!

SCOTT

(Handing Jackson the phone.)

Order something.

JACKSON

No please?

SCOTT

It's been a week and since no one is fucking...

(*Frank chuckles.*)

...while you are here, you are now the head chef in the sexless Burnem house.

JACKSON

You could always go to your place, Scott.

FRANK

Well...

SCOTT

I sub-letted it for the rest of the month...

JACKSON

That why your shit is in the bathroom, huh?

FRANK

Just learn to plug your ears or go home, Jack.

JACKSON

She won't pick up the phone, you know that, Frank.

FRANK

Maybe try a house call.

JACKSON

Alright, messaged received. What I am ordering Chinese or Pizza?

FRANK/SCOTT

Chinese.

JACKSON

Wow. Adorable. You're fucking...nesting...

(*He starts to dial and stops.*)

Should I bring flowers?

FRANK

Monica hates plants. She feels too responsible for their death.

JACKSON

Candy?

FRANK

Monica hasn't eaten sugar in 12 years…

JACKSON

What should I…

(The door flies open revealing Monica. Jackson sighs and sets down the phone.)

Hey…there she is…

MONICA

Outside. I need to talk to you.

JACKSON

Great, I'm about to order Chinese.

MONICA

In private, Jackson.

JACKSON

Frank's as good as private.

MONICA

(Leaning into the room a bit.)

Hi. You must be Scott? Nice to meet you…well not meet…I've…

SCOTT

Right. The lovely wife, I've heard nothing but good things about…nice to…meet you.

MONICA

Frank.

FRANK

Monica.

MONICA

Jackson.

JACKSON

Scott. Are we all clear now?

MONICA

Jackson, please…

JACKSON

Please, what, Monica? Spill the beans, I have a hunch.

MONICA

Are you serious, right now?

JACKSON

7 years, Monica, you'd think you'd be able to recognize my fucking serious face.

MONICA

Can we not, in front of…

JACKSON

In front of who, Monica? I've been sleeping on their fucking sofa…

SCOTT

He said 'their…'

FRANK

Welcome to the family, shut up.

JACKSON

…because you won't answer my calls. I had to go to a fucking showing meeting in dirty fucking clothes because I couldn't go home and change because my wife, my dear wonderful fucking wife, wouldn't let me inside! So, please, whatever you need to privately say to me, say it now, Monica because shit is already awkward as…shit!

FRANK

I have a washer, Jack.

JACKSON

I have no idea how to use it, Frank!

(A long silence)

MONICA

I slept with Richard.

SCOTT

Who the fuck is Richard?

FRANK

Richard Kroachivelli?

JACKSON

Well, there's that, then…

MONICA

Yeah, there's that.

FRANK

Monica…

MONICA

Oh, fuck off, Frank.

(She leaves and slams the door. A long pause.)

153

FRANK

You…can stay until…

(Scott sighs and lights fade on area.)

SCENE SEVEN

(Jackson sits on Frank's sofa, sketching. An off-stage argument is heard.)

SCOTT

(OS)

It's insane! If I didn't know how tragically straight…

FRANK

(OS)

Which is why *this* is insane. It's my best…

SCOTT

(OS)

I have friends too Frank. I'm just not spooning them…Do you chew his food, Frank? Spit it into his mouth for him?

JACKSON

(To himself.)

Well…I wonder who they are talking about…

FRANK

(OS)

Your friends wouldn't mind the spooning…If anything I should be worried about all your friends…

JACKSON

Nice…

SCOTT

(OS)

Wow…

FRANK

(OS)

Wait…Don't…it's…

SCOTT

(OS)

I can't keep delivering your messages.

JACKSON

Shit…

FRANK

(OS)

What?

(*Scott enters the room and stops, acknowledging Jackson.*)

SCOTT

You've got a pretty good friend in there. Almost too good, kind of creepy good…

JACKSON

We get that a lot. Listen…

SCOTT

No, that's enough. Enough of listening to *you*. Good luck, Jackie.

(*Scott goes to exit, Frank enters.*)

FRANK

Don't slam the…

(*Scott slams the door.*)

FRANK/JACKSON

…door.

(Frank sits next to Jackson.)

JACKSON

You alright?

(Frank glares at Jackson.)

Right.

FRANK

(sighing.)

So what do you want? Thai or pizza?

JACKSON

Frank…

FRANK

Jackson, I am hungry, what do you want?

JACKSON

Thai…

FRANK

Wonderful. Number 12 no onion, right?

JACKSON

Right…

(Frank begins to dial.)

Frank…

FRANK

What?

(*Jackson takes the phone*)

You want pizza now?

JACKSON

I want...to tell you something.

FRANK

Fine. I feel like I need more heart to hearts today. Not Pad Thai, apparently, just heart to hearts...Shoot.

JACKSON

You...remember a few years back when you had that show?

FRANK

At the basement?

JACKSON

Yeah, you had this...painting of...some crap of a self. Bunches of Chotchkies lined up.

FRANK

It was called Vestiges. It was...we collect so much meaningless objections, which only mean something to the owner...

JACKSON

...the owner, yeah I got it.

FRANK

You hate it?

JACKSON

The general idea, sure...but...it's my favorite thing you've ever painted.

FRANK

You stopped me from ordering noodles to tell me that you hate the subject matter of...your favorite of my paintings?

JACKSON

Yes.

FRANK

You're an asshole, Jack.

(Frank takes back his phone and goes to dial again.)

JACKSON

Frank the noodles can wait, listen to me.

FRANK

Jackson, I have spent my primary existence listening to you, what is so damned important that you want me to sit here…alone and hungry…

JACKSON

I think the painting is brilliant. I think you are brilliant.

FRANK

I don't need you to patronize me because my boyfriend stormed…

JACKSON

…I thought you weren't subscribing to any titles…

FRANK

Whatever. Just don't…patronize me.

JACKSON

I'm not. I was just telling…someone that the shadows on that piece are…they are perfect. I could never do that. I tried once. I…it's brilliant. You should paint more.

FRANK

Thank you.

JACKSON

I just thought someone should tell you, that the shadows are really great.

FRANK

(*chuckles.*)

What the fuck, Jack?

JACKSON

What?

FRANK

You trying this whole talking bullshit. It doesn't suit you, just stop it. Who put you up to it? Scott tell you I need an ear?

JACKSON

No, I just thought…

FRANK

(*angry.*)

Thought that I what? That I needed you?

JACKSON

Maybe…I don't, I thought, I should try to…

FRANK

Fuck. I don't need you, you need me. You need me, Jackson. You need my sofa. You need my advice. You need me to fucking show you how a washer works…I don't need you. I *needed* a life. I needed a companion. I *needed* to get laid. But it's never in the cards, is it, Jack? I fucking married you. Didn't I? I married you. And we all know I can't fuck you! Monica got out, I'm still fucking stuck. I am not getting laid or getting noodles because I am fucking stuck…

JACKSON

Let's go to a gay bar. Find you a nice…

FRANK

I am not going to a gay bar…

JACKSON

Wear those jeans, the tight ones I got you…

FRANK

I am not wearing tight jeans at a gay bar with you…

JACKSON

You look like a young Eric McCormack…

FRANK

Who? Damnit, Jackson, shut up!

JACKSON

Maybe get me drunk enough…

FRANK

Jokes. Always a joke for it.

(Frank stands and goes to the door.)

I'll be back later.

JACKSON

Sure.

FRANK

I over-heard the whole fucking thing last week…

JACKSON

(Frank goes to leave.)

Fuck. Frank, I'm…

(Frank slams the door.)

…Sorry.

(Another confessional spot appears, this time, revealing Scott.)

SCOTT

I have lived my life placing myself into situations where the acceptance would come hard. Be it over-priced dance academies, or relationships. My piece de resistance became Frank Burnem, a man who's walls are almost palpable in the air around him. I've watched Frank and Jackson through hundreds of lunches. Lunches about Monica. Lunches with Monica. Lunches about weddings. Divorces. Bad reviews. Bad blood. Apologies. There's been tears. Hugs. A punch was thrown and plates have been broken, but never once, a lunch that I could assume was the last. Their attraction seemed unshakably permanent. And, as much as I wanted to hate the fact that this adorable, clearly gay, regular never sat alone, I found it sweet. I found his need to repair Jackson's every wound like a broken childhood toy…just adorable. Every time Jackson's arm fell off, Frank would sew it back on, kiss the boo-boo, and send his creation back into the world, stronger and better than when they came in, for yet another lunch. Frank may have missed the boat as a painter, he may very well be a seamstress with the ways he's sewn his friend back together. In watching their exchanges through the years, in seeing them change, age, go through some terrible hair, I fell maddeningly in love with the man who was clearly, already, taken. Frank was in love with every lunch. In love, and addicted. I was addicted too, obsessed with being the 3rd wheel on their 2-wheeled cart. I stayed too long at their table, catching up, hearing what they were up to, expecting no tip. I wanted this charming, sad, sweet man to sew me up. I wanted to cry to him over onion rings. I wanted him to listen to me. To want me. To notice me. I wanted half of the composition. Only half. I think that maybe I always knew that I was never going to be able to repaint the scene, and perhaps that is my comfort in choosing to fall for the most unobtainable men. It's protection. It's never having to let my guard down. It's never getting too comfortable. Never. It's raising my father from the grave and creating an army of men, all waiting to deny me and walk right out of my life. I don't know how many times I left my number on napkins, but it took him forever to finally call. And when he did, he called, late and drunk. Something had shaken his very core and he wanted to get out of the apartment that was full of reminders of a man he could never have. So, I picked him up, at 11 at night, and we went to a bar, where I could buy him more drinks and buy myself more time with the half of the piece I wanted. The whole night he kept sadly repeating the same phrase, "People just don't get him, like I do." He said it with sadness, with pride, and with a sense of duty. The same sick mantra: "People just don't get him, like I do." This toxic friendship was how he defined the very "I" in that sentence. Frank sees himself as the cereal box decoder ring and Jackson as the code. Before we kissed he not-so-jokingly asked if I was sure I was gay. Hours before I closed the distance between myself and the custumer of my desires, Frank closed a distance between himself and Jackson. It was the kiss to end any hope in him that the man on the end of the table would ever be more than a duty. More than an addiction. That night, I gladly auditioned to be his Jackson stand-in. I gave him the love he'd never get from his broken childhood toy. Then, I broke. I broke from months of stress. Months of jealousy. Months of being second and stood up. Months of being looked through. And, Frank didn't sew me back up…he hasn't even called.

(Lights out.)

(Frank is sitting in a robe on the phone. Jackson walks in.)

JACKSON

(Showing Frank some papers)

Look Frank! Birthday divorce papers!

(Frank puts up a finger to silence Jackson.)

FRANK

(on the phone.)

I understand that, it's just…

(Sighing.)

You're right. No. You're right. And Martin…

(Jackson looks appalled.)

JACKSON

No…

FRANK

Where? Why? Vacation from what? Alright. I will. I'm…no. I'm not seeing anyone. I'm not…banging a waiter. Martin… he says a lot of things…I'm hanging up. I am…Dad?

(Tossing his phone onto the table.)

He hung up.

JACKSON

So, who called?

FRANK

You know who called.

JACKSON

And you didn't let me talk to Dad?

FRANK

God no. He hates you.

JACKSON

How's your brother?

FRANK

On vacation. So, I am...doing his spreads for June...

JACKSON

Frank, no! You are fucking kidding me!

FRANK

Let's see those papers.

JACKSON

No. These very legal documents are no longer important. What is important is the most talented artist I know doing spreads for a sports rag. Isn't June the bikini body countdown? What the fuck are you doing spreading bikini bodies?

FRANK

I need the money and I need to do something, Jack. I can't keep guilting you into take-out...I need...I'm bored, Jack.

JACKSON

It's fine. You're fine. I have money, I have plenty of money. Fuck, I owe you plenty of money. If you are bored paint some Chotchkies, you don't have to...

FRANK

Let me see those papers, you might not have much money after signing those...

JACKSON

Frank did you give up?

FRANK

On what?

JACKSON

On being an artist.

FRANK

A long time ago, gimme…

(Jackson hands Frank the papers and Frank starts to go through them.)

JACKSON

Why?

FRANK

Art destroys you and I don't have time for both of us to be destroyed.

(Handing Jackson the papers.)

Happy Birthday, by the way…How old are you this year? Still 29?

JACKSON

I'm 34.

(A pause.)

FRANK

You're 35.

JACKSON

Either way. Do you think I am destroyed?

FRANK

You're a wreck, you don't know who you are anymore.

JACKSON

Fuck, Frank. Way to lighten the mood…

FRANK

You barge in here wielding divorce papers and blame me for killing the mood. People don't want the next great artist anymore, Jackson. They want the next Grand Theft Auto.

JACKSON

I can't believe that. Somewhere, probably not in America, but somewhere there's one kid reading about Picasso who sucks at video games.

FRANK

Not so sure about all that, Jack.

JACKSON

Come on, Frank. It's not like I think I am ever going to be a Picasso, Van Gogh, Warhol…I'm not…there's not going to be pictures of me in text books…but I have to believe that…someone gives a shit…

FRANK

That's nice.

JACKSON

Frank, Frank, Frank. I never expected you to fly. No one did. I knew we were going to be toys falling with style. That's the thing with modern art; You can't fly anymore, you've just got to resolve to fall. But always with style. With purpose. And damnit, put on a fucking show. Get falling, my brother, just put some finesse in your decent.

(A pause.)

I can't have you just giving up on me, you're better than that.

(Sitting.)

Besides, we'll always have each other?

FRANK

Oh God, I hope not, I hope I reserve myself the dignity for suicide before I am sitting opposite you in the sun room of a home…

JACKSON

(Sarcastically taking Frank's hand.)

But, Frank. I love you.

FRANK

You shouldn't lead people on, Jackson, it's rude and unbecoming. Let go of my hand.

JACKSON

Fuck! Look at us! Is this what we had in mind?

FRANK

How drunk are you?

JACKSON

Rather.

FRANK

I smell that.

JACKSON

Should I sign these?

FRANK

It's your life, and, in this case your wife and I can't make this decision for you.

JACKSON

Frank you make all my decisions for me. What should I do?

FRANK

(frustrated.)

I don't know what you should do, Jackson. And I don't know what I should do about you. I don't know what I can say to Monica to make her love you again. I don't know what I can say to Scott to make him come back. I don't fucking know Jackson. I literally don't even know how I fucking got here.

JACKSON

You walked down 10th.

FRANK

And we're joking about it. Always laughing about it. It's easy to laugh at Frank's plight, isn't it? You know what, Jack, I do know how I got here. And please, allow me to take a moment and describe to you what 'here' looks like. It looks like this shitty apartment. It looks like doing spreads for my father and my brother, whom I can't stand. It looks like alone. It looks like jerking it in the shower for another 15 years. It looks like all the shit in my bedroom that I have to get back to the guy who stormed out on me. It looks like me, Jackson. Look at me. I look old. I look tired.

JACKSON

Frank, you're adorable, I'd be on my knees in front of you right now if I was gay, I swear I would.

FRANK

God damnit, Jackson let me finish…

JACKSON

Not inside me, Frank. I've seen Rent…

FRANK

(screaming.)

Damnit, Jackson, stop!

(Both are silent.)

You're how I got here. You.

JACKSON

What?

FRANK

I want a divorce.

JACKSON

Oh, you too?

FRANK

Yeah, Jack. Me too.

JACKSON

You couldn't have given me sometime between divorces. It's my fucking birthday, Frank.

FRANK

No. Don't you do that. Don't you fucking do that. Don't you make me the bad friend. I was never anything but the best friend to you. Above and beyond, Jackson. People think I am insane. People don't get it. People don't get you. It's exhausting…you're so…exhausting.

(Jackson stands up, angry.)

JACKSON

Exhausting? Let me explain something to you about exhausting, Frank. Exhausting is feeling guilty every damn day for not taking dick. Exhausting is feeling bad for getting married. Exhausting is feeling bad for being single. It's every time you give me that look and we both know exactly what it means: It means I have to be sorry. It means that I get to spend another day feeling bad for not sucking you off, that's fucking exhausting.

FRANK

You're an asshole. I didn't ask…

JACKSON

I didn't ask!

FRANK

You didn't ask what?

JACKSON

I didn't ask for you to love me. But, let's be honest, It's because I have such a great ass isn't it?

(Frank punches Jackson. Knocking him to the ground. Frank instantly grabs his hand.)

FRANK

Shit! That hurts…

JACKSON

You know, Monica never hit me…

FRANK

Get out.

JACKSON *(he stands.)*

You're not a saint. You've stolen from me. You've mocked me. Used me to look like the saint you aren't. You put down my work. You don't want to see me succeed because if I did…you wouldn't have to take me home and dust me off…I'm not your masterpiece, Frank.

FRANK

Don't make me hit you again.

JACKSON

I won't…I can't fight for shit.

FRANK

Leave.

JACKSON

Let me just…

(He goes to the table and collects his divorce papers.)

Get…these…bye Frank.

(Jackson exits.)

FRANK

Alright.

(He sighs.)

OK…

(He sits. Lights fade on area. Once again the confessional style lights pop up.)

JACKSON

Frank is obsessed with Mark Tansey, an artist, known for painting these almost grey scale monochromes of daily scenes. His most famous, Frank's favorite painting on this Earth, is a piece called Four Forbidden Senses, an awful title, featuring a bathroom scene of women in depressing grey blue. One smoking, one spraying…perfume or Lysol, I was never sure. Either way, by the time I was in college, Tansey's ship had really set sail into the forgotten distance. Shockingly, people weren't into the short lived post-modern color studies of the early 80s, anymore. And like most artists fading from glorious month-or-so long fame, Tansey, began making guest lecture appearances around art schools, inculding ours. During my end of term ritual of doing most of my work the night before it was due, Frank, once again, spent the better part of 24 hours with me trying to salvage my portfolio. He never told me that all the while, tickets for this precious Tansey lecture were dissipating. When the stupid thing finally rolled around, I asked Frank who the lucky lady, yes I knew better by then, on his arm would be. During the 23 hours Frank spent trying to save me from failing out of Beginning Oil Painting, the lecture had become amazingly over-sold. I guess that further proves that Frank has always had better taste than me. Despite everyone's assumptions of me, I did feel awful. I spent the next week tracking down pairs of tickets and trying to make deals in alley ways like I was buying drugs. I finally tracked down two tickets, unfortunately resting in the hand of Nancy Gladstone. Nancy Gladstone had had an obvious crush on me since our meeting in Drawing 2 and although the unibrow worked for Freda Kahlo, it did not work for Nancy. The events that followed are not to be accounted to those with a faint heart. I am quite sure it was only when faced with my deplorable selfishness that I let myself face the simple fact that Frank, 2 years my senior, would be graduating in a mere handful of days and that there would be nothing keeping him from leaving New York, really. Except, maybe, me and those tickets. I started making points to walk with Nancy after class. To sit with Nancy at meals. To let Nancy's boney hands rest on my leg precariously close to other parts of my anatomy. One night I even took Nancy to the movies, I'm not proud of myself, but I was blinded by a cocktail of fear and guilt. That night, while we held hands back to her dorm, I explained my fears to Nancy, and the gift I had planned for my friend. I'm a very charismatic lair. Not a skill I meant to foster, just a skill that in my life, has fostered itself and a skill that landed me two tickets to Mark Tansey…fairly easily. The price of her relinquishing those tickets came at…well…I didn't go back to my dorm that night. I left in the morning feeling dirty, a little sore, hung-over, and a bit like a prostitute. I assumed everyone I passed that day knew, but I had in my back pocket, my salvation. I met Frank for lunch, as was customary and could tell he was clearly excited to tell me some sort of great news. He informed me that because Monica was president of…let's be honest most of the student clubs…she was able to get him a single pass into this riveting 3 to 4 hour lecture. Suddenly, my take for the team became useless. I could feel the bland cafeteria food settling heavy in my stomach. I never told Frank. I never told Monica. And I never explained to Nancy why I just slipped the tickets back into her mail shoot. Because, it's easier for everyone to blame me. It's easy to be mad at me. To think I am selfish, to think I don't hear my disclaimers when I am introduced. It's easier, far easier, for me to be hated, than to be loved.

(Lights out.)

(Jackson, now with the pinkish reminder of a black-eye, sits on a paint covered sofa, reading a review in an art gallery. Scott enters.)

SCOTT

They really didn't like this one, huh, Jackie?

JACKSON

(reading.)

A confusing and offensive step back into old habits, Jackson Bell never fails to disappoint as an artist…

SCOTT

Ouch…

JACKSON

…In asking his audience to take part in interacting with painted sofas, Bell has gone a step farther from disappointing us, and has flat-out insulted his audience by asking them to join his miserable, lonely and self-centered existence. If someone asks you to attend this tragic display by Bell, politely decline and enjoy the sofa in your own home…

SCOTT

It's beautiful, you should have it framed.

JACKSON

Fuck you…

(Scott sits on the Technicolor sofa with Jackson.)

SCOTT

So they didn't get it…

JACKSON

This was the nicer review.

(He tosses the paper on the ground.)

My career is over.

SCOTT

It's not...

JACKSON

Scott...

SCOTT

You may never paint in this town again, Sweetheart.

JACKSON

I'll have to move. I don't know how to do...anything else.

SCOTT

Then, you might be a real artist.

JACKSON

I might be.

(Laughing.)

How the fuck are you, Scott?

SCOTT

I'm horribly, tremendously miserable. And you? Adjusting to the single life?

JACKSON

I've gained 10 pounds in take-out and I fear that I am starting to smell.

SCOTT

Well, you look like shit.

(Jackson chuckles.)

JACKSON

Thanks.

(A long pause.)

You haven't…

SCOTT

No. I have not and I haven't tried.

JACKSON

Four months on my own and I've managed to destroy my reputation as an artist…completely.

SCOTT

I'm surprised it took you this long.

JACKSON

(Holding up his ring hand.)

Two. Two in one year, Scott.

SCOTT

At least you still have your ass.

JACKSON

You're alright. Thanks for coming.

SCOTT

I had to see the most hated display of the season.

JACKSON

Here she is…

(He motions to the space.)

SCOTT

Did she…

JACKSON

Of course not.

SCOTT

You know, Jack, there's a certain art to living. Maybe your esthetics are just changing.

JACKSON

I should tuck you in my pocket and let you be my little fabulous little Jiminy Cricket.

SCOTT

(He takes the handkerchief from Jackson's suit pocket, refolds it and replaces it.)

You could stand a queer eye.

(Frank enters with a program from the show.)

Why look, I sprinkle a little fairy dust and I brought you a little Christmas miracle.

JACKSON

It's June, Scott…

(Seeing Frank.)

Well. You look like shit.

(Scott stands.)

SCOTT

You might want to fix that, he's a wreck.

FRANK

Oh?

SCOTT

Look at that composition. Totally one sided. And he's getting fat.

FRANK

Alright…

(Frank lingers.)

SCOTT

174

Oh, stop it, you have my number.

(Scott exits and Frank goes to sit opposite of Jackson. They sit in silence for a bit.)

FRANK/JACKSON

I love you.

JACKSON

Wow. I hope no one heard that.

FRANK

Fuck, I hope not.

JACKSON

It dies here.

FRANK

It's dead.

JACKSON

I don't even know what we are talking about because it is already dead to me.

FRANK

You really do look like shit.

JACKSON

So do you.

FRANK

How...

JACKSON

On some days I can't get out of bed, others I barely eat. So...better.

FRANK

I know what you mean.

JACKSON

I do.

FRANK

Do what?

JACKSON

Love you. Just not…

FRANK

I know.

(Both sit quietly for a moment.)

I like it.

JACKSON

You do?

FRANK

Sure, it's all you. It's loud, it's offensive, it's over saturated, there's not subtlety or shadow, I think it even made a woman in the first room cry. It is undeniably yours.

JACKSON

Damned reviewers should have asked you for some jabs…

FRANK

It's honest.

JACKSON

No reason to lie. Sofas. My whole life revolves around sofas. It's been a year of fucking sofas…

FRANK

Year of the Sofa.

JACKSON

That *is* better.

FRANK

What did you call it?

(Jackson flips the program in Frank's hand over. Frank reads.)

I'm Sorry.

(Jackson shrugs.)

FRANK

It's as obnoxious as you are, but it's got a good core. That's what makes a piece good, Jack. Who cares if the colors are wrong, it's the core. It's the core of a thing that has to be good. Not shadows or themes. The best art doesn't need anything but an honest, good core.

JACKSON

It was like I forgot how to paint. Nothing on canvas worked and when I got home…all that was left was that fucking white sofa with that tiny red stain and I couldn't help but think that nothing in my house, maybe nothing in my life, was ever meant to be so God damned white…

FRANK

God, no. White stains.

(Jackson laughs.)

I'm glad I saw it.

JACKSON

Last night, really made me wait, you fucking diva…

FRANK

I wanted to make sure, I don't know. I just wanted to be sure…

JACKSON

I know.

(A pause.)

Frank. Tell me you're sorry for punching me in the face on my birthday the day of my divorce.

FRANK

Never.

JACKSON

Lunch?

FRANK

I'm buying?

JACKSON

I'm ruined.

FRANK

(standing.)

Come on. She never...

JACKSON

She never. Can we please get the fuck out of here?

FRANK

We're going somewhere dark, we look like shit.

(They begin to exit.)

I want to show you something...

JACKSON

Yeah?

FRANK

Piece I am working on. I want to see what you think.

JACKSON

You painted something?

FRANK

Yeah. I didn't want to just…give up.

JACKSON

Good.

(They go to exit. Jackson stops, looking back at the sofa.)

You know, that one was our sofa.

(Frank laughs.)

FRANK

You're an asshole, Jack.

(Both exit together. Monica enters carrying a program for the showing and stops at the sofa. She checks it over, flips a cushion and finds a paintbrush. She sits for a moment and places the paintbrush back in the cushions. She then stands on the sofa, as the lights fade. The stage once again turns into two tight spotlit areas.)

FRANK

It has to do with our pasts…

JACKSON

And our futures.

FRANK

With our dreams…

JACKSON

And our nightmares.

FRANK

With holding on…

JACKSON

And letting go…

FRANK

But never…

JACKSON

Forgetting.

FRANK

For now…

JACKSON

Forever.

FRANK

Into the future…

JACKSON

While remembering our pasts.

FRANK

And finding out why.

JACKSON

And accepting how.

FRANK

Coping with the addiction.

JACKSON

Learning how a washer works…

FRANK

Forgiving.

JACKSON

Forgiving.

FRANK

It's changing…

JACKSON

Yet, it's always the same…

FRANK/JACKSON

Art.

PART III

Canvas

Canvas, the final play in the series, will premiere at the 2017 Indy Fringe Festival. The play welcomes former *Portraits* cast member, Adam Tran, as director.

- Jackson Bell played by Davey Pelsue
- Frank Burnem played by Dave Ruark
- Martin Burnem played by Matthew Walls
- Monica Graham played by Afton Shepard
- Scott Miller played by Nathan Thomas

This play is dedicated to the dear friends stepping in and returning to this world. Sometimes the end is just the beginning, and I am thrilled this play's production story began with each of you. The painting is complete.

PROLOGUE

(Lights up on area, where, Frank and Jackson, two-artists and best friends, stand in two down-facing spotlights, ready to address the audience.)

JACKSON

Art...

(Frank is silent and Jackson seems distressed by this, just then, the lights suddenly blackout. In this darkness, the sound of an ambulance is heard. When the lights return Jackson and Martin, Frank's brother, sit in a bleak and sterile looking room. Jackson paces around what we now see is a hospital waiting room, Martin sits and taps his foot, rapidly.)

JACKSON

What the fuck are they even doing in there!? You know? We're out here...waiting...just fucking waiting...and they can't fucking come out here and tell me what's going...I mean they call it a fucking waiting room. Am I right? A *waiting* room. A room made for fucking waiting. What a sick god damned joke...

MARTIN

Fucking language, asshole.

JACKSON

Martin, if you have to fucking open your mouth again, can I please ask that it only be to insert my cock?

(A pause. Martin scoffs.)

Shit...would you look at this fucking room we've built and decorated with vinyl chairs and fucking non-offensive, overly pleasant sunset, flower and bird art, I use *art* loosely, here...

MARTIN

Of course you do…

JACKSON

My cock, Martin, do you remember my cock? Your mouth is open—I assume you want a taste…

(Suddenly, Jackson has an angry outburst, kicking a chair.)

Christ…I mean…we're fucking waiting…you can't find a second to come out here and…What the fuck you are doing in there!?

MARTIN

(Robotically.)

They're trying to get my dead brother's heart going…

(Noting Jackson.)

Dick…

JACKSON

Don't.

MARTIN

Don't what?

JACKSON

Don't say dead.

MARTIN

I can say dead.

JACKSON

(Dangerously quietly, angry.)

No. You fucking can't.

MARTIN

(Standing, getting very close to Jackson.)

I think I can do as I God damned please, *Van Blow*.

JACKSON

Hit me.

MARTIN

It would be my pleasure.

JACKSON

Then fucking hit me.

MARTIN

I'm not going to give you the hard-on.

JACKSON

This isn't my fault.

MARTIN

Isn't it?

JACKSON

So fucking hit me.

MARTIN

No.

(Jackson sadly sits.)

JACKSON

Well, you've changed.

MARTIN

(He laughs and sits beside Jackson.)

You haven't...much.

JACKSON

Fucking cock-sucking Christ, what do *we* talk about!? What do *you* and *I* talk about...in the *waiting* room?

MARTIN

How about how I banged your wife before you got the job done?

JACKSON

Ex wife.

MARTIN

(Jackson chuckles.)

Something funny?

JACKSON

Good one.

(Jackson runs his hands through his hair. He makes a small sound, perhaps about to cry, he then hides his face in hands. Martin glances over at the scene and hesitantly pats Jackson's shoulder. Just then, Scott, Frank's on-again-off-again boyfriend, runs in. Martin lifts his hand from Jackson's shoulder as if caught in the act of something horribly wrong or as if Jackson's shoulder is suddenly scalding hot. Scott, still in pajamas, but wearing a jacket and tennis shoes, looks around quickly trying to find a familiar face.)

SCOTT

Jackie?

(Jackson, face still hidden in his hands, raises only an arm, like a school kid, while Martin stands and moves toward Scott, with his hand awkwardly extended and smiling entirely too much.)

MARTIN

(Sudden and too chipper.)

Hi!

(Going for a handshake.)

You must be...

SCOTT

Yes! The…brother?

MARTIN

The brother. The ah…*boyfriend?*

JACKSON

Seriously, Martin, don't even fucking try to understand it…

SCOTT

We're not…it's—

JACKSON

Don't fucking open that box, Martin. Let me tell you about a bitch named Pandora…

SCOTT

(To Martin.)

We've never met…you two weren't close.

MARTIN

We aren't. We only get together on…special occasions.

(Martin motions to the room and Jackson laughs through a sob, still talking into his hands.)

JACKSON

Martin, I don't remember you being this funny. Hi, Scott.

SCOTT

Jackson.

(Scott sits with Jackson.)

JACKSON

(Lifting his face, addressing Martin.)

Sit the fuck down, Baboon.

MARTIN

Fuck off, Prick-caso.

(Martin sits.)

SCOTT

Have we heard…?

JACKSON

Nope.

SCOTT

What did he…?

(Jackson breaks his hug with Scott.)

MARTIN

This asshole's fucking pills…

SCOTT

Pills?

(To Jackson.)

Really?

JACKSON

Oh, comeon! Not like…for *insomnia*…I left them there during the divorce…

SCOTT

Was he?

JACKSON

Drunk.

SCOTT

Wow. How Requiem for a Queen…

(*Martin laughs.*)

JACKSON

(*Chuckling.*)

Marty, I'm really glad we got to do this.

MARTIN

Me too.

JACKSON

(*Jackson wipes some tears from his face and sighs, sitting up.*)

How's it going, Scott?

SCOTT

Why don't you tell me—

JACKSON

Right.

(*A pause.*)

SCOTT

I bet he didn't even get the good shit.

MARTIN

Cutty Sark…

(*Scott and Jackson laugh.*)

MARTIN/JACKSON

(*Sighing.*) I fucking hate that shit…

SCOTT

He may have impeccable taste in men, but no one ever claimed him to be a scotch connoisseur…

JACKSON

I missed you, Scott.

SCOTT

I've been around.

JACKSON

Oh, I've heard.

SCOTT

I'm sure you have.

JACKSON

(Yawning.)

He wishes he could quit you...

SCOTT

Find him a new cowboy and he can.

MARTIN

I don't get it...

SCOTT

Honestly, honey, I wouldn't expect you to...

JACKSON

(Professorially.)

You see, Martin, as far as cock gobblers go, your brother is apparently something of a premium grade...

MARTIN

Jesus. Don't...

(Scott chuckles.)

SCOTT

It's good to see you. Not like *this* but...

JACKSON

Don't ever stop fucking my friend, Scott. I'd hate to have to choose my reigning Queen.

SCOTT

Don't know if I can really keep that promise to you, now, Jackson, in light of the present events…

JACKSON

Don't act so high and mighty.

SCOTT

I guess you're right. He was dead inside when we met.

(Martin smiles. Jackson chuckles.)

MARTIN

And Frank says he doesn't have a type…

(Jackson laughs, regards Scott and smiles. There is a pause.)

JACKSON

How are you guys?

SCOTT

I don't fucking know, Jackson…

JACKSON

He loves you.

SCOTT

(Scott makes a sound that could be the onset of crying. Then sighs, centering himself.)

Sometimes, I just want out of your little soap opera…

JACKSON

If he wakes up, I'm hitting him…

SCOTT

Second.

MARTIN

And *I'm* the caveman.

JACKSON

Cavemen painted. You're more of a Neanderthal.

MARTIN

Cunt...

JACKSON

Not your best.

SCOTT

(Monica runs in, looking frazzled.)

Oh, wonderful. You got the E-vite!

(Jackson laughs.)

MONICA

People don't E-vite anymore, Scott, they Facebook. Where is he?

(Jackson points off-stage, into the hospital halls.)

JACKSON

Purgatory?

(Scott and Martin laugh, heartily.)

MONICA

(Angrily.)

What the fuck is wrong with you? Frank's...

JACKSON

Frank's dead.

(Blackout. When the lights return, as suddenly as they went off, Martin remains, alone, to address the audience.)

MARTIN

I don't normally do—alright: I remember when Frankie was like 17 years old and he decided to come out to our dad. Not…like…come out of the dick-sucking closet—just like come, *clean*, really. Or, as clean as he was ready to be. Frank had just gotten home from school and he rushed to set up a manila envelope of…I don't fucking know, report cards? Sketches, acceptance letters—who ever knows with Frank, he's—he's a genius. He had this fucking tray of refreshments on the table, lit goddamned candles, even…It was like he was trying to romance our fucking father. That always struck me weird. And sad. Dads should already be on your side; there should be no romance. So, Dad gets home from work, late—to see Frank sitting at the dining room table with a spread of candles, that had now burnt down into these pathetic little waxy pools next to a manila envelope of convincing—I'm sure—arguments…

(A pause. He's pained.)

I'll never forget it. It…ah…hurt? Dad, without sitting down, groaned, "Well Franklin—" I know, Franklin, he was doomed from the fucking start. "What do you want, then?" and Frank took in this deep breath and calmly—but that fake kind of calm when your voice is still a little shaky—said, "Dad, I want to go to art school." I'm not even really sure why, but I remember wincing for Frank after he had said it. Dad didn't say anything. Then, he just started *laughing*, this really deep hearty laugh that we had never heard before. And then, I think just to feel included, Frank started laughing too—But I was actually the first to know *why* we were laughing…Frank going to art school was ridiculous. A joke. Everyone in the Burnem bloodline knew that Frank had received an early acceptance to Stanford for engineering, not art. Frank was going to be an engineer and he was going to get his pesky art fetish taken care of interning for Dad's magazine. See, we—the Burnems, didn't talk about *art*. That evening, the men shared a long laugh, then, without real warning, dad blew out what was left of the candles and he walked away. And Frank sat alone with stale snacks in the darkness and no definite sense of approval. I think shit like that always hurts. But what the fuck do I know?

(Lights fade, sudden, on area.)

SCENE ONE

(Jackson packs a suitcase in a hospital room full of belongings that look more like Frank's than his own. He looks a bit messy, messier than usual, as if he's been sleeping at the hospital. Martin enters with paper work, looking much fresher than Jackson.)

MARTIN

Where's…?

JACKSON

Bathroom.

MARTIN

Cut the cord long enough to let him take an innocent piss?

JACKSON

I haven't blinked in 4 days, Martin, don't fucking push me.

MARTIN

You sure? I mean…he's my brother…I should—

JACKSON

Mine, too. Basically.

MARTIN

If you're sure…

JACKSON

(Quickly changing the subject.)

All checked out?

MARTIN

All checked out.

(Frank enters; he looks tired and a little vacant.)

FRANK

Martin?

MARTIN

Martin.

FRANK

(Tapping his head.)

Getting there.

JACKSON

Don't stress yourself out. Not over Martin…

MARTIN

Fuck you.

FRANK

You really could have gone home.

JACKSON

(*Stroking Frank's cheek, jokingly.*)

And miss watching you sleep? Never.

FRANK

Don't…touch me.

JACKSON

(*Shocked.*)

Sorry.

FRANK

It's just…I don't *really*—know

JACKSON

Oh, you do know…too well…you just don't remember. It's okay, Drew Barrymore, we'll get you caught up.

FRANK

What?

JACKSON

Drew Barrymore, she's a popular film actress, she was in this shit-show called 50-First Dates…the girl has some disorder where she can't remember Adam Sandler…wish I had it—it made Monica cry, well, she was wine drunk, really wine drunk, but still…*you* loved it. Jesus, you're a blank slate…

FRANK

I know who Drew Barrymore is.

MARTIN

He hates that movie.

JACKSON

Shut the fuck up, Marty! I want to reset him a little. Where's your sense of fun?

(Frank looks concerned and glances over to Martin.)

MARTIN

Hey, you picked him, Bro.

JACKSON

(Patting Frank on the shoulder.)

You're stuck with me. It's sort of our thing.

FRANK

Alright.

MARTIN

(To Frank.)

They need your ID out front. And your signature…like a thousand times, I'd imagine.

FRANK

Alright.

(Frank looks over to Jackson, for permission.)

JACKSON

Get out of here. I can't believe I'm about to say this, but I've officially had it sleeping on sofas.

MARTIN

Congratulations.

JACKSON

Fuck off, Martin.

(To Frank.)

Go on. Get—

(He gives Frank a playful shove to the door.)

FRANK

Don't touch me…

(Frank exits. Jackson sighs and sits on the bed, sadly folding a shirt, mumbling to himself. Martin sits beside him.)

JACKSON

(Mocking Frank.)

Don't touch me…

(Jackson sighs.)

MARTIN

Going once, going twice…

JACKSON

I'll be fine.

MARTIN

Jackson…

JACKSON

I'm fine.

MARTIN

I can't believe I am about to say this, but…call me, if you need to talk.

JACKSON

Gross. It's only going to be a couple days; he should be normal in a couple of days. Well, Frank. He should be *Frank* in a couple of days…

MARTIN

You look tired.

JACKSON

My eyes fucking hurt.

MARTIN

You have to blink sometime.

(Martin stands and goes to leave.)

JACKSON

Martin…

(He seems like he's about to make yet another classic 'Jackson crack', but he thinks better of it.)

I'll…keep you posted.

MARTIN

Thanks. Hey—shit changes…

JACKSON

Like art.

MARTIN

I'll take your word on that, Van Blow.

JACKSON

Thank you.

(Martin puts a hand up to high-five Jackson, Jackson answers by rising his own.)

Ape Boy.

(They somberly high-five.)

I think you're evolving.

MARTIN

Hey, Jackson?

JACKSON

Yeah?

MARTIN

Seriously, fuck off.

(Jackson laughs. Lights fade on area.)

SCENE TWO

(Lights up on Jackson's apartment. Frank sits in an uncharacteristic, ill-fitting and tight band T-shirt and sweat pants, doodling something. Jackson enters carrying shopping bags.)

JACKSON

(Overly-chipper, sarcastically mocking the situation.)

Honey, I'm home! Cue *The Odd Couple* theme! Fuck baby, do I love coming home to you…

FRANK

Hey…

JACKSON

(Walking through the room and back off-stage into the implied kitchen to put down the bags. He mocks Frank as he re-enters.)

Hey…

(He sighs and tosses a small bag onto Frank's lap.)

Here. Got you this. Flowers seemed too much.

FRANK

(Frank pulls a book from the bag.)

Brave New World?

JACKSON

Yeah. It's one of your favorites. Which is fucked up in it's own right...

FRANK

Thanks.

JACKSON

(Sounding too excited.)

You're drawing?

FRANK

Bored. Not everything is gone...just the 'whys,' 'hows' and 'whos.'

(He motions to the sketch.)

But this, it's like...

JACKSON/FRANK

Instinct.

JACKSON

Maybe we could go by the studio later? I'll show you this piece I'm working on...if you're up to it. I need your instincts to rip it apart for me...I'm stuck—I just keep staring at the tits...

FRANK

Maybe I'll love it.

JACKSON

Not if you are using your *instincts*. Ripping my work apart is as natural to Frank Burnem as breathing. You're an art critic, after all. Nice shirt, by the way. It's good and...tight.

FRANK

Yours?

JACKSON

Mine. You hate The Flaming Lips.

FRANK

I wasn't really paying attention, I just grabbed something from…

JACKSON

(Smiling.)

The dryer? See, I learned! Look at me, Franklin, I am a beautiful fucking butterfly. A laundered fucking butterfly.

FRANK

What?

JACKSON

Never mind.

(He sits with Frank and looks at his sketch, making a confused then, almost disappointed face. Frank smiles at his reaction.)

FRANK

Why are we friends?

JACKSON

You've always wanted bang me and I needed my thesis written. Simple as that.

(Jackson stands to leave.)

FRANK

Simple?

JACKSON

Sure, simple.

CASEY ROSS

(Standing, grunting with a hitch in his knee, and going to put away the rest of the groceries.)

But—only in the initial conception of the piece—we let it get complicated, over time. Time changes concepts and conceits…

FRANK

Hey, Jackson?

JACKSON

(Stopping.)

Hey, Frank.

FRANK

How deep was the cut when I came to and didn't know your name? Was it Lifetime movie bad? Did you cry a little? Martin told me you cried.

JACKSON

Jesus fucking Christ, Frank…

FRANK

Oh, come on, laugh…

JACKSON

That wasn't funny.

FRANK

It was.

JACKSON

Too soon.

FRANK

My fucking suicide joke, Jackson, you don't get to critique it. I'm the critic, right? Besides, you love 'too soon.'

JACKSON

204

I do love 'too soon'…

(Jackson, a little happy in the banter, sits back down with Frank.)

FRANK

Martin said—

JACKSON

Fucking ape… *(sighing)* yeah, alright, Frank, yeah…I cried. Happy?

(Frank smiles, but it quickly fades.)

FRANK

No. And I thought I would be…

JACKSON

Fuck, Frank. You make me feel like Anne Sullivan.

FRANK

Jackson Bell *is* The Miracle Worker…

JACKSON

(Playfully shaking Frank.)

Banter, Frankie! Banter!

FRANK

(Serious.)

Thank you.

JACKSON

Hold on to that. Once it all comes back to you, I want to have some leverage. I have years of shit I'm still making up to you.

FRANK

You look exhausted.

JACKSON

I'm okay.

FRANK

No you aren't. You're a terrible liar. Your honesty is adorable.

JACKSON

(Standing.)

Yeah, that shit's all instinct, too…

FRANK

Figures…

JACKSON

Aw, what the fuck…

(Jackson hastily hugs Frank. Frank seems shocked but finally participates in the hug.)

What the fucking fuck, Frank?

FRANK

I couldn't sleep. I just wanted to feel—I…I tried feeling *new.*

JACKSON

You should have called me.

FRANK

And what about that would have been new?

JACKSON

Not much. Maybe…the talking, like really talking…I don't know. What the fuck does feeling new even mean, Frank?

FRANK

(Squirming out of the hug.)

206

Let go.

(A long pause. Frank looks over at the dejected Jackson and smiles.)

JACKSON

(Seriously.)

I need you, Frank…

FRANK

What do you need, Jackson?

JACKSON

Huh?

FRANK

What do you actually need from me?

JACKSON

You. What is this? What are you doing?

FRANK

I'm *talking* to you, Jackson. Really talking. I'm talking and it's just not what you want to hear.

JACKSON

Alright, Frank, let's dance…

FRANK

Bring it.

JACKSON

I need you, Frank. I need *you*. That's what I'm supposed to say, right?

FRANK

Look around, Jackson! You don't need me, anymore! This is your place, isn't it? I'm crashing on *your* sofa now, aren't I?

JACKSON

Sure…but…

FRANK

(Tugging at his shirt, making it an example.)

You washed this? Dried it?

JACKSON

The dryer's kind of broken…so—

FRANK

It was damp.

JACKSON

How damp?

FRANK

Just damp, let it go. You—you grew up, Jackson. You love Pete's Dragon, I'm sure you're smart enough to make the fucking connection.

(Jackson sighs, giving up the argument.)

JACKSON

I do love Pete's Dragon. And that's a pretty direct metaphor, Frank, no connections to make. Fuck, I *do* love Pete's Dragon.

FRANK

And 'too soon.'

(Jackson smiles noticing that Frank's remembered something specific about him.)

JACKSON

Look at that…

(A pause.)

How damp?

FRANK

(Sighing.) It's…it's wet.

JACKSON

Frank—

FRANK

Oh, stop. Jackson, if I had died, you would have kept living. Simple as that. You would have kept painting. You would have kept being…Jackson. What am I without you?

JACKSON

You're Frank.

FRANK

And who the fuck is that?

JACKSON

I don't have an…you're *Frank*. You…read pretentious books…and paint still-lives. You iron your shirts even when you have nowhere to go. You know the right ways to do…everything…like poaching eggs. I could have never poached an egg without you, Frank. You're gay…and you totally hate that. you're…you, Frank. You're Frank…you're my fucking friend.

FRANK

I'm *your* fucking friend…

JACKSON

(Standing, again.)

No. You're *Frank*. Read your book, I'm taking a nap…

(Jackson exits. Frank sighs.)

FRANK

(He picks up the book from Jackson, flipping to a random page and reading.)

"If one's different, one's bound to be lonely."

(Lights fade on the area.)

(Lights up on area. Scott and Monica sit at a café, both looking tired. Monica picks at a plate, Scott drinks tea.)

MONICA

Have you been over?

SCOTT

No. Called…

MONICA

I just…I mean what do I say? And I'm *not* calling Jackson…

SCOTT

I feel like I should give him a break.

MONICA

He won't take the help, Scott. He's…you know exactly how he is. How they both are…

SCOTT

Stubborn, co-dependent, toxic, disgusting, a little sweet…need I say more?

MONICA

Jackson and Frank: The rest of the world is just their fifth wheel…

SCOTT

Monica, if you are going to continue to sing to this choir, I'd pray you'd pick a better song…

(Monica laughs.)

MONICA

Hey, I was the Third Musketeer first, you really took my crown.

SCOTT

And you're welcome to have it back. You hear that? A queen relinquishing a crown, it must be a dark day.

MONICA

(*Checking her watch.*)

Why am I not surprised?

SCOTT

Don't say anything.

MONICA

I would never.

SCOTT

I know. The ice queen is just a character you do.

MONICA

I still love him. I still love both of them, I just can't live *with* them…

SCOTT

Here comes that song again…

MONICA

I'm sorry.

SCOTT

It's fine. What else would we talk about?

MONICA

My God, they're the center of the universe.

SCOTT

We're giving them everything they want.

MONICA

So, you called?

SCOTT

I called. I just called. That's all I've done… *is call.*

MONICA

How did that go?

SCOTT

How do you think it went? I asked him if he wanted me to take a shift, he swore…stubbornly…that he was fine. Funny thing about it is, you can literally hear how *not* fine he is in his voice. He sounded pale.

MONICA

How does one sound pale, Scott?

SCOTT

You lose your color. We talked till he fell asleep.

MONICA

About?

SCOTT

Easy things. Artists he hates. Good paintbrush brands. Big Brother…

MONICA

Jackson doesn't watch Big Brother…

SCOTT

That was when he fell asleep.

(*Jackson enters the diner, already talking, hastily.*)

JACKSON

I'm shit! I'm shit! I'm shit and I'm never on time! Just trying to cover all the bases here guys…

MONICA

I didn't say anything.

SCOTT

Well, if you had it would have been bordering on trite.

MONICA

Don't be a bitch.

SCOTT

Don't be a bitch. Sit down, Jackson.

JACKSON

(Sitting.)

Did you order for me?

SCOTT

Jackson, you've been ordering the same thing for the past 8 years.

MONICA/SCOTT

Number 7, no onions, black coffee…

SCOTT

—Of course, I ordered for you.

JACKSON

See? I make it easy because I *know* I'm going to be late.

MONICA

You could just learn to keep time…

SCOTT

Monica!

MONICA

(Frustrated.)

I'm not saying anything!

JACKSON

You know what, Monica? I was going to be on time today, had it all planned out. Really, I did. You know why, Monica? Because I wanted nothing more than to prove you wrong and shove it in your resting-bitch-face!

(Scott laughs, causing him to spit tea on the table.)

MONICA

(To Scott.)

Charming.

SCOTT

Don't be a bitch.

JACKSON

I got held up at Martin's…

MONICA

Well, aren't you two just best friends, now?

JACKSON

Sure are, we love getting together and picking the icicles off our dicks.

(He sighs, trying to compose himself.)

I'm really fucking tired, Monica—be cool.

MONICA

How is he?

JACKSON

Foggy, but fine.

SCOTT

How are you?

JACKSON

Oh, God. This is my intervention, isn't it?

SCOTT

We think you might be hooked on the stuff…

JACKSON

Well, at least I'm *on* him, not *in* him.

SCOTT

I gave you that one.

MONICA

(Rolling her eyes.)

You're stronger than I am, Scott…

JACKSON

Certainly more faithful…

MONICA

You know what, Jackson? I'm letting that go. I'm working on that—letting go—with my therapist…

JACKSON

Your therapist, *awesome*…

MONICA

…Working on letting go and working on getting *through you!*

JACKSON

There it is! Couldn't really let it go, could you, Monica? Had to get one in, didn't you? What's your fucking therapist say about *that?* O.K., come on! The walking target's here now, shoot away! Fucking shoot away, Monica!

SCOTT

Easy, there, Jackson, you *are* hard to miss…

JACKSON

Who's fucking side are you on, Tiny Dancer?

SCOTT

I think I've asserted that I'm not on anyone's side...

JACKSON

Just their *insides*?

SCOTT

Now you're stretching...

(Jackson smiles, about to retort.)

Don't!

MONICA

Stronger than I, Scott...

JACKSON

Well fuck, aren't you two just a couple of Christian martyrs?

SCOTT

Why are we bringing Jesus Christ into this?

JACKSON

You can be any kind of martyr you'd like, Scott...

MONICA

We are in public...

SCOTT

Like this is the worst I've witnessed at this very table...

JACKSON

Since when did we care so much about the fucking public? *(He sighs, lowering his voice.)* I'm done. Monica? Done? Can we all just be done?

(A long pause. Monica takes some mail from her purse and slides it across the table to Jackson.)

MONICA

Have you filed your change of address, yet?

JACKSON

Nope, I'm so helpless I couldn't even manage the US Post without you.

(Sighing.)

Monica, it's been final for 3 years. I've filed my change of address.

MONICA

Well, Richard found those in the box.

JACKSON

Richard?

MONICA

My husband. You know who Richard is.

JACKSON

Oh! *Kroachivelli?* Richard Kroachivelli the dog-artist, must have slipped my mind! His work's so…cute. So, he's in my mailbox now, too? Wow, that guy is just getting into all my boxes, lately…

SCOTT

Jackson.

JACKSON

Ok. Alright, guys, what do you want me to do? Take a bubble bath? A walk? A therapist, would that work Monica? Would a therapist work?

SCOTT

Jackson.

JACKSON

So, what do I do, guys?

SCOTT

Jackson…

JACKSON

That's my fucking name! I know we're all busy being the most concerned, but my best friend just tried to kill himself. Do you get that? Like the only real tangible partner I've had in my life—the one thing I hadn't totally fucked up—just mostly—tried to off himself. Pills, booze, *and* a noose, he meant it. He's a triple threat in suicide and if he makes it another year, he'll probably remind me that suicide is yet another thing he's fucking better at. So answer me this: what do I do, guys? Maybe you didn't hear me; Frank just tried to kill his-fucking-self—

SCOTT

And that's not your fault, Jackson…

JACKSON

Wow. That old cliché, Scott? Fuck you, you don't believe that bullshit.

MONICA

Jesus Christ, Jackson, listen to him…

SCOTT

No, he's right.

JACKSON

Jackson's always doing all the listening, all the changing. Not today. Today, you two are going to listen to me: This *is* about me. It's about me. It's about Frank. It's about us. This is not about—

SCOTT

I do go inside of him, from time to time…remember?

JACKSON

Fine Scott, inner-Frank issues are all your business. Monica, you can stay the fuck out of it.

MONICA

We're worried about you, asshole!

(Jackson sighs. Scott stands, pours Jackson a coffee and returns to the table.)

JACKSON

Scott, you don't work here, anymore.

SCOTT

I do not.

MONICA

Sorry I called you an—

JACKSON

Don't be…I am.

SCOTT

Jackson, you are many things, and only one of them is an asshole. I just don't want to see you get used. Especially not used *up*. Alright, you're a painter: You know how expensive a good Titanium White is?

JACKSON

$34.99.

SCOTT

When something is that valuable, you use it sparingly. I'm not sure you or Frank Burnem ever learned *sparingly*. You with your colors, him…with you. Now, go home and tell that clingy queen that he should pack a bag and stay with his brother. Or his boyfriend. Or his parents. It's not only you, Jackson Bell. It never had to be. It wasn't fair…

(Patting Jackson's cheek.)

It's not fair, Jackie.

(He slides Jackson's coffee to him.)

And drink this, you sound pale.

(Jackson takes a sip of coffee; Monica hesitantly places her hand in Jackson's as the lights fade on area.)

SCENE FOUR

(Lights up on Jackson's flat. Frank sits reading the book previously tossed in his lap by Jackson. Jackson enters, seeming a bit shaken.)

FRANK

Long lunch.

JACKSON

I went for drinks with Scott…

FRANK

Ah.

JACKSON

Fuck off. We didn't talk about you…

(A slight pause.)

We totally talked about you. That man *loves* you, Frank.

FRANK

I know.

JACKSON

'I know?!' Listen, you queer Han Solo, I mean he *really* loves you. If you could just—

FRANK

Stop loving you?

JACKSON

That…

FRANK

Are you drunk?

JACKSON

I think the answer to your question is fairly obvious, Frank.

(*He trips and falls into his coffee table.*)

FRANK

Christ, you smell like a gay bar, stop…moving. Here—comeon…

(*He helps Jackson to the sofa.*)

JACKSON

I love you too, Frank.

FRANK

I didn't say—

JACKSON

You did, once…

FRANK

10 years ago.

JACKSON

(*Genuine shock.*)

You don't love me anymore, Frank?

(*Jackson starts running a hand through Frank's hair. Frank laughs.*)

FRANK

No, Jackson, unfortunately I live in the exact converse of that situation…

(*Lying Jackson down on the sofa in less mobile position, covering him with a throw blanket. This is a habit for both of them.*)

JACKSON

You do still love me? I knew what converse was. Smart! I'm a real catch, Frank. Scott said we should…

FRANK

Scott said what? That we should talk about our feelings? Let's not. Not with you like—

JACKSON

(Sitting up, demanding.)

No, now, I'm ready now—Scott said I should—what do you love about me?

FRANK

(Attempting to stand, Jackson catches him and holds him down.)

Loved. 10 years ago, Jackson…can we, please—

JACKSON

(Sitting up and firmly holding onto Frank's arm, keeping him from leaving, but still genuine.)

Please what?

FRANK

(Weaker.)

Can we please not open this wound, Jackson?

JACKSON

I'm not trying to open your *wounds*, Frank…

(Jackson puts his hand on Frank's leg.)

FRANK

Jackson…

JACKSON

(Flirtatiously, moving toward Frank.)

You still love me, right?

FRANK

I think you know the answer to that.

JACKSON

(Moving closer to Frank.)

So, am I hot, Frank? Is that it? Like I'm just super hot to you gays—

FRANK

Jackson, please—why would you ever do this? Why—how could *you* ever actually do…*this.*

JACKSON

What am I doing wrong, Frank? Don't you want me? Just tell me what I'm doing wrong—

FRANK

I swear I could fucking choke you…

JACKSON

Kinky…

(Jackson leans onto Frank, kissing him, for a few moments this develops. After a moment, however, Frank begins to struggle, then suddenly pulls away. He punches Jackson, hard.)

JACKSON

Fuck! Again!? I knew my ass went to shit…

FRANK

Get up.

JACKSON

Are you going to hit me again?

FRANK

Maybe. Get up.

JACKSON

Give me a second. Fuck, you throw a good punch…and you're not a bad kisser.

FRANK

Leave.

JACKSON

(From the floor.)

It's my place, Frank…

FRANK

I don't care.

JACKSON

(Reaching to Frank.)

Frank…I'm—

FRANK

Don't fucking touch me!

JACKSON

I'll—I'm sorry, Frank listen to me…I didn't mean—I just…I didn't know what to do, okay? I thought I lost you. You're the only person who's ever loved me…ever…and I can't lose that and I thought I lost it…If I could just—if I could just…please listen to me, Frank…

FRANK

You aren't making any sense.

JACKSON

Frank—please…

FRANK

You're straight, Jackson.

JACKSON

I'd try—for you…if I could just…

FRANK

You're fucking straight!

JACKSON

Frank, come here…calm down…

FRANK

I've spent *years* accepting that, Jackson. Years!

JACKSON

Please—

FRANK

I spent *years* leading Scott on…you remember, Scott? That nice guy you went out drinking with? That man who loves *me*, the guy that I hurt almost every single day by not loving him right?

JACKSON

How the fuck do you love someone *right*, Frank?

FRANK

I don't know, Jackson, I just know I'm not doing it.

(A pause.)

JACKSON

I just thought you didn't love *me* anymore…And I—wanted to keep you.

FRANK

(Smirking in disgust.)

Keep. Love. Love you. Love *you*? You!? You, you, you, you, you, you, you! Always *you*, Jackson! Of course, I still fucking love you! Loving you is why I still fucking exist!

JACKSON

That is not true—

FRANK

(He rolls his collar down showing a reddish mark on his neck.)

Isn't it? Why don't you take a look at what loving you did...

JACKSON

Please, stop...

FRANK

Look at it.

JACKSON

Frank...

FRANK

You're fucking straight.

JACKSON

(Whispering, looking down.)

You're right.

FRANK

Look at me.

(Jackson obeys.)

Say it.

JACKSON

Why—?

FRANK

Say it. Look me in the eyes and say it or I swear I'll hit you again.

(Jackson obeys.)

JACKSON

I'm straight.

FRANK

And you're fucking drunk.

JACKSON

But I still love you, Frank. Scott said—

FRANK

Fuck you, Jackson Bell.

(Frank grabs a coat from the coat rack.)

JACKSON

Frank, that's not your—

(Frank exits, slamming the door, Jackson flinches at the sound.)

God dammit.

(Jackson, still on the floor starts to cry. He picks up a remote from the coffee table and flips something invisible on. Music begins to play. Preferably Elton John's 'Your Song.' Jackson crawls onto the coffee table and lies on it, face down and weeps quietly as the lights fade on the area.)

SCENE FIVE

(Lights up on Scott's apartment, It's a studio very small, but bright, lit warmly by candle light. Scott sits on a loveseat watching what sounds like dance, and also flipping through a dance magazine. There's a firm knock on the door.)

SCOTT

(Calling to the door.)

It's open.

JACKSON

You really shouldn't just leave your door unlocked, Scott, this is a rough neighborhood.

SCOTT

Oh, Jackson, you just aren't used to being a bohemian anymore, come in. Besides, I have drag queens who need to borrow my old dance costumes at these hours, it's an open door policy. Tea?

JACKSON

(Very edgy.)

Can I stay here tonight?

SCOTT

I thought you'd never ask, baby.

(Standing, patting the loveseat and exiting into the kitchen to retrieve a cup of tea.)

Sit down.

JACKSON

Scott, I'm a piece of shit…

SCOTT

(Real concern.)

Jackie…what happened?

(Jackson starts to cry. Scott exits but quickly re-enters with tea and hands it to Jackson. Jackson fails to take the cup.)

JACKSON

I kissed Frank.

SCOTT

When's the wedding?

JACKSON

Scott, I'm so sorry…I—piece of fucking shit, Scott…I just—how can anyone do this alone?

SCOTT

Do what?

JACKSON

Live. How can anyone do that alone? I need him…I—need

(He trails off. Scott smiles and joins him on the sofa, patting his shoulder. He hands him the teacup again.)

SCOTT

You smell like a gay bar.

JACKSON

That's what he said. That bar does make a fucking brilliant mojito.

SCOTT

Told you so. Drink your tea.

JACKSON

You hate me now…

SCOTT

Oh, please, I already did. Drink your fucking tea.

(Jackson obeys. There's a pause.)

You know, Jackie, I've kissed other boys…

JACKSON

Does Frank—?

SCOTT

Does Frank think he has a monopoly on my tongue? Yes, probably. Does he know I've kissed other boys? Also, probably. Sip.

(Jackson, starting to calm down, does so.)

Jackson. Frank's selfish.

JACKSON

What?

SCOTT

Oh, he's got you whipped bad, doesn't he?

JACKSON

Frank's not—

SCOTT

Oh, you are his masterpiece, you might not ever see it. Frank wants it all his way, and he makes it so. Frank wants to stay miserable, so for you to be with Frank…in your whatever you two are way, you have to be miserable with him. At any cost. He's been keeping at this game for years, Jackson. Frank Burnem has a better life than most queens painting sad still-lifes in New York should have…

JACKSON

How do you figure?

SCOTT

He's had you! Every step of the way. A *real* friend. When you saved that bitch from getting his ass kicked in the schoolyard after art class—and let's be honest Jackson, I am sure he had it coming…

JACKSON

He called the guy's final an artistic abortion in uninteresting tone theory…

SCOTT

Deserved it.

JACKSON

Yeah, totally.

SCOTT

And you saved him on the playground and he—literally—fell for you…or *on* you…

JACKSON

We were in college, thank you. And I fell on him.

SCOTT

Whatever. When you threw that punch, you didn't do it to hurt anyone but the guy kicking the shit out of a poor art-fag with glasses. You didn't do a thing wrong to Frank Burnem. You just tried to help him not get his teeth knocked in, then, he fell in love with you, Jackson. And that's not your fault; he just treats you like it is.

JACKSON

Maybe.

SCOTT

Frank is so lucky. He's had a real friend—a friend who's loved *him* not because of any tongue monopolies but because to you—through some divine connection…Frank Burnem *sparkles*. You look up to him like he's just shimmering, Jackson. Like he's the goddamned sun. You believe you can't do anything without him, but you can do anything with him. I would have killed to have a man ever look at me the way you've look at Frank Burnem your whole life. And Frank's never noticed *that*. Frank sees things in ways to stay miserable. He sees what he can't have in you, not what he has always had. Fuck fucking, Jackson. So, you're straight?

JACKSON

I think so…

SCOTT

(Looking over Jackson.)

Yeah, honey, you're straight.

(Jackson chuckles.)

So poor Frank will lose your *worship* for *sex*? Fuck fucking. I'm sorry to tell you, Jackson, but not seeing your worship for the loss of a lay…that's fucking selfish. It's selfish for Frank to make you feel guilty for not letting him suck your dick. Especially when, all the while you've been sucking his…in your way.

JACKSON

Wow.

SCOTT

Tea.

(Jackson sips, then suddenly speaks.)

JACKSON

So he is a bottom?

SCOTT

Sometimes. I'll get you a blanket.

JACKSON

Frank's lucky you care about his sugar, Scott.

SCOTT

Frank's lucky.

JACKSON

(Nearly whispering.)

Thanks, Scott.

SCOTT

Hey, I think I'm kind of stuck with you too now, you come with the package…so—drink your tea.

(Beginning to exit.)

You two are going to kill me, darling, and I used to dance for Madonna. Vogue Tour.

JACKSON

Frank never told me that.

SCOTT

He's appalled.

JACKSON

Frank's an idiot.

SCOTT

Who knew you and I tend to agree?

(Scott watches Jackson staring sadly into the half-drank tea for moment then, stopping just short of leaving into his bedroom he hastily rushes to Jackson, kissing him. Jackson fumbles, spilling the tea, shocked.)

Yeah, I don't get it.

(Scott tosses a blanket at Jackson, ruffles his hair and exits into his bedroom. Jackson laughs and pulls the blanket over him, and lies down, as the lights fade on the area.)

SCENE SIX

(Lights up on Jackson's condo. Martin sits on the sofa, watching television. He seems sluggish. Jackson enters.)

MARTIN

Jackson.

JACKSON

Shit, you've finally come to kill me. Martin, how in the fuck did you—

(Martin holds up keys, showing Jackson how he got in.)

Right.

MARTIN

I was sent here for Frank's crap…

JACKSON

His books?

MARTIN

Yeah, I didn't know what belonged to which of you fags in here…

JACKSON

And, then you figured you'd just take a fucking break?

MARTIN

Yeah, actually.

(He removes a joint from his pocket and lights it. He takes a hit and hands it to Jackson.)

You smoke, Dick-vinci?

JACKSON

Not your best. And no.

MARTIN

Shut up, here.

JACKSON

Oh, I'd rather not extend this…

MARTIN

(Suddenly pointing at the TV.)

Poop!

(He removes a beer from his jacket pocket, opens it and toasts to no one, chugging.)

JACKSON

(Glancing over to the TV.)

Hoarders…Hoarders Drinking Game. Frank teach you?

MARTIN

Drink twice for dead cats. I will give you butt-pirates this; this is a damn good drinking game. Sit the fuck down, Jackson.

JACKSON

I'd rather watch my ex-wife bang her marketable prune, Martin.

MARTIN

It's a good one. Your favorite. Fridge Cats.

JACKSON

Fucking Fridge Cats?

MARTIN

All 34 of 'em.

JACKSON

Did you bring beer?

MARTIN

(Standing and exiting for the kitchen, motioning for Jackson to sit.)

Have a fucking seat, Jackson…

(Jackson moves to the sofa and sits, heavily. Martin returns with a round of beers. In silence, the men open their beers and click bottlenecks and Martin takes another hit of his joint.)

Nice place, you have here, Jackson…really…

JACKSON

Please stop trying.

MARTIN

(Handing Jackson a joint from behind his ear.)

Fine. Here.

JACKSON

Believe it or not, Martin…I really don't—Fuck it.

(He takes the joint from Martin and takes a hit, coughing.)

MARTIN

Aw, Van Blow's a rookie…

JACKSON

I'm paranoid enough as it is, Martin…I don't usually aim to expedite it.

(Martin looks confusedly at Jackson.)

Speed it up. That's what expedite means.

MARTIN

Just talk like a normal fucking person, Dick.

JACKSON

I'll limit my vocabulary for this…event.

MARTIN

Thank you.

(Martin takes a hit, and hands it back to Jackson who rolls his eyes, doing the same. He, again, coughs.)

So. How are—?

JACKSON

How do you fucking think I am, Martin? I assume he told you everything—

MARTIN

He actually doesn't talk to me, Jackson. Hasn't in a long time.

JACKSON

You don't know what happened?

MARTIN

Didn't even ask.

JACKSON

I kissed your brother.

MARTIN

Fuck. Well, here, I promise you Frank's high as shit, right now…

JACKSON

Frank doesn't smoke—

(Martin laughs.)

MARTIN

Yes. He does.

JACKSON

You think?

MARTIN

I know. We smoked all the time, in high school, when we were working on my cars.

JACKSON

When you were what?

MARTIN

Frank's an engineer, Jackson…he can fix a fucking fuel pump. That shit makes *no* sense to me.

JACKSON

Martin, what are you saying? It sounds like gibberish.

MARTIN

Frank fixed my Chevy in high school. And you know how Frank feels about Chevy's…

JACKSON

He has an opinion on them at all?

(Frank walks into the room, followed by Monica, and tosses a set of keys on the table.)

FRANK

Might as well have bought a fucking Ford, Martin.

MARTIN

I almost did. Hey, Monica.

MONICA

Do not fucking speak to me, Pig.

JACKSON

She used to talk to me like that…

MARTIN

Good to see you too, dear.

FRANK

Martin—

JACKSON

(To Martin.)

She's the best, isn't she?

MONICA

Frank…

FRANK

Could both the pigs stop rooting in the mud long enough for me to pick up my things?

JACKSON

It's a box of books and some clothes, Frank, it didn't take all this and you know it.

FRANK

I wasn't coming back here alone.

JACKSON

(Jackson scoffs.)

Yeah, okay.

MARTIN

(Stretching, opening a beer and beginning to talk as if not tension has been added to the room.)

You know, I'm sorry I even asked you, Frank. You're going to make it a thing aren't you? *(To Jackson)* He's so dramatic. Are you going to fix my fucking car? *(To Jackson.)* My car's down—

FRANK

What the fuck are you doing, Martin?

JACKSON

Seriously, what the fuck is going on?

MARTIN

My car won't start.

MONICA

We get that.

MARTIN

I thought we weren't talking.

MONICA

Frank, get your fucking clothes.

JACKSON

Alright, so what does Frank have to do with your transmission?

FRANK

Get it all out, Jackson…

JACKSON

I will. You can fix his car?

FRANK

Yes. I can.

MARTIN

How old were you when you built that motor?

FRANK

Martin…

MARTIN

What? Your butt-boy—

JACKSON

I'm not his…

MARTIN

That's not what I heard.

MONICA

Did you two kiss, again?

FRANK

CASEY ROSS

(To Jackson.)

You told him?

JACKSON

(Sadly.)

It bothers me Frank…all I do is tell people and apologize.

MONICA

Oh god, did you fuck?

JACKSON

Monica, please, we just made out.

FRANK

Hardly.

JACKSON

All I do is apologize, Frank…

FRANK

Good.

JACKSON

This isn't necessary, Frank.

(Scott enters, surveys the situation and sighs.)

Hi Scott.

SCOTT

Place looks great, Jackie.

JACKSON

Thanks.

(Monica sits down.)

240

MARTIN

Christ, come on, Frank. Your butt-boy—

FRANK

He's not…

MARTIN

He will always be your butt-boy and you know it. And your butt-boy should know he's more of a fag than you are…so, come on…how old where you when you built that motor.

SCOTT

I think I like you, Martin.

JACKSON

I do, too. Oddly enough.

FRANK

14.

MARTIN

14, that's right.

FRANK

I have dexterous hands.

MARTIN

That's what I heard from Liz.

FRANK

Fucking drop it, Martin…

MARTIN

Never.

MONICA

Can we go? Please get your fucking clothes, Frank.

SCOTT

You know that's not why we're here.

JACKSON

Who the fuck is Liz? How fucking high am I?

(Martin hands the last of the joint to Jackson who takes a hit and coughs. Frank smiles at this, then recovers back to a neutral expression before being 'caught.')

MARTIN

Alright, Van-Blow, listen to this—

FRANK

What are you two friends, now?

MARTIN

You've made your point, Frank, let me make mine.

FRANK

Excuse me?

MONICA

Frank—

MARTIN

You just hold onto things, for-fucking-ever, no end—no forgiveness…give him a break, Frank. Look at him.

FRANK

I don't need to look at him. I can paint him from memory.

SCOTT

Oh, Jesus…

(Scott joins Monica, sitting. There's a somber, tense pause. Martin removes a new beer from his pocket and opens it, taking a long chug, then crunching the can, setting it on the table, hard—for effect.)

MARTIN

Our mother caught Frank...red-handed, you could say...

JACKSON

This Frank?

MARTIN

That Frank. Frank and Liz were supposed to be doing homework in the basement and Mom goes down there to find Frank finger banging—

FRANK

Jesus, Martin...

MONICA

You're a pig.

MARTIN

You're a bitch.

(Jackson laughs.)

Finger. Banging...the captain of the girl's soft-ball team...

JACKSON

Jock girl. Nice.

(Scott laughs.)

FRANK

Fuck you, Martin.

SCOTT

Be nice, I want to hear the story.

(Monica chuckles.)

MARTIN

Get the stick out of your ass, Frank.

JACKSON

(Sadly, without looking up to Frank's reaction.)

That's probably where he wants it…

(Martin smiles, and holds a long moment of eye-contact with Frank, choosing to continue his story.)

MARTIN

Ass like a ripe cantaloupe, Jackson, I'm telling you. So of course, Frank tries to pretend nothing was going on…

FRANK

Martin—please.

SCOTT

(To Monica.)

I get why you fucked him.

(Monica smiles and shrugs.)

MARTIN

This is literally the best story in the world, he deserves to hear it, Frank.

SCOTT

You're brother's awesome, baby.

FRANK

Alright, fuck it. It's not like I really have dignity anymore…

MONICA

Oh, stop.

(Frank sits with Monica and Scott.)

MARTIN

Frank claims nothing was happening, except his left hand…

JACKSON

He is a lefty…

SCOTT

Yes, he is.

FRANK

Don't.

JACKSON

I don't even want to fucking know…

MARTIN

Left hand, covered in blood. Liz got her fucking period while Frank was, from what I heard—doing some excellent finger work…

MONICA

Oh, god…

SCOTT

Please, we're all girls, here.

JACKSON

No—

MARTIN

Oh, yes, Van Blow. Frank swore to mom that it was paint.

JACKSON

Frank Burnem, I am honestly impressed.

FRANK

Don't talk to me, Jackson.

MARTIN

I can't believe you never heard that one, Prick-caso. What in the fuck have you two been talking about for the last 20 years?

(*Jackson and Frank both shrug. Martin stands and picks up a box of Frank's items and starts to exit.*)

Maybe that's part of the problem then, Dicks. Come on.

(*Martin exits. Monica and Scott hesitantly stand.*)

MONICA

Are you going to be—?

JACKSON

No. I'm not.

MONICA

Jackson—

SCOTT

(*Pulling Monica along with him.*)

Let's—

(*He nods to Frank and Jackson who are locked into an awkward eye contact.*)

MONICA

Alright.

SCOTT

See you later, Jackie.

(*Scott and Monica exit.*)

JACKSON

Frank, I am so…

FRANK

Don't.

(Frank takes a couple sweaters from the coat rack and exits. Lights fade on area. A sudden tight spotlit area appears and Jackson enters it, addressing the audience.)

JACKSON

I realized something the other day: The most awkward feeling I had ever sat through with Frank Burnem wasn't kissing, or long talks late at night, or taking an incorrectly loaded gun away—It was post his graduation when he was no longer my TA. It was the freedom. It was knowing that we were no longer just assistant teacher and student but simply…friends. It was knowing—deep down, that Frank stayed for me. That Frank was…mine. It was sitting next to Frank on his off-campus couch, while he longingly starred at me…being able to touch me—even by the school rules. It was me being curious to see when the attempt would happen. It was simply…forever different. I wouldn't have graduated undergrad without him. It's always been the joke within our little group. How Frank wrote my thesis—how he loved me so much he selflessly put his reputation as a T.A. on the line to save my grade in Advanced Studio Visual Arts. That's painting for the layman. Everyone knows that story…and it's true. Some frat boys thought I sucked his dick to get him to agree to it…that's much less true. What people don't really know is that he also did my Sculpture final for me, and that was a *self*-portrait. He did all my Mixed-Media projects. And Photography. And he wrote every single paper I bothered to turn in for art history. Frank really went through art school twice, because all…I've ever been able to do is paint. You see, I *am* a painter. Just a painter, nothing more. That's why I've never gotten what he sees in me. I can't hold down a job, sustain a marriage, or make stovetop macaroni. I barely do laundry. I can't sleep, I take pills for that. Can't sing. I can't really run that fast. Can't fight for shit. No sense of style. I'm pretty sure I smell like paint thinner. My hair's a mess and when I stand next to him, as complete as I've been able to make myself, I'm still *half* the man he is. Half the *person* he is. Who the fuck is Frank? How could he ask me that? I *know* Frank. I just don't know who the fuck *I* am. I know what I do. I paint. But, that's all I do. All I am. If breathing didn't keep me conscious, I might not even find an escape for doing even that. And then, poor Frank would have to do even that for me. He keeps asking me what he is: He's a teacher, he's a friend, a lover, an avid reader, he's a damned good cook, he can sing—I've heard it. He's a genius. He can paint. His shadows…matter, they mean things. He's exact but you can shake him. I can make him laugh. And he can do everything. He loves me? Me? I just paint. I'm *just* a painter—and he's even better than me at that. He's my *hero*, not my friend. My *hero*. I should probably tell him that. Scott said I should probably tell him that…

(Lights fade on area.)

(Lights dimly up, in Jackson's bedroom, it's still messy, but it's become eerily more adult, as if to say Jackson's grown up as best he can. Frank bursts in, sudden, through the door, in pajamas, he looks frail.)

FRANK

Jackson.

JACKSON

(Waking, putting on glasses that were once seated on the bedside table.)

It's 5:52 A.M., Frank.

FRANK

I have something to say.

JACKSON

Well, then I think you have to say it.

FRANK

We were sitting in the cafeteria…

JACKSON

In college?

FRANK

Jackson, shut up. We were in the cafeteria. You were eating that unappetizing off-brand Skyline chili, and I wasn't eating. And we were talking about something completely mundane; something that I can't remember and that I don't care to. Because…Jackson, the thing I can't forget is that you smiled…at me. And it was crooked and it trusted me. And it broke through all the walls I had ever built. And I loved you. Dearly. And I refuse to stop. I tried to stop. But now, I refuse to, because at night when I cry myself to sleep, because I want nothing more than to stop loving you, I think about you smiling at me, and I know that's the best thing that's ever happened to me. You, smiling, with chili in your beard. It was the moment that I knew why I was on this Earth…and for a while, knowing why was enough. I was made to love you, Jackson Bell. That's why I tried to kill myself.

JACKSON

Shit.

FRANK

Yeah shit, Jackson.

JACKSON

How did you get in here, Frank?

(Frank holds up his set of keys.)

Right. Frank—

FRANK

Jackson.

JACKSON

(Hopeful.)

Will you ever forgive me?

FRANK

I don't know if I can.

JACKSON

What if I throw some chili in my beard?

FRANK

Stop it.

JACKSON

I'm sorry. Frank, sit down.

(He pats his bed.)

Please.

FRANK

You aren't trying to seduce me again, are you?

JACKSON

Please sit down. I'll keep my hands on top of the covers, I promise.

(Frank sits on the bed, next to Jackson.)

I want to tell you a story Frank. But I don't have a brother to do it for me. Fucking jock girl, Frank…

FRANK

Stop it.

JACKSON

O.K. See, Frank…you're who I have. You took me home for Thanksgiving in school, Frank. You've never met my father, have you?

FRANK

No.

JACKSON

So, I'm sorry Frank, I've got to be the one to tell you this: But, 2 weeks ago, you were with Scott, and I was here, and I was flipping through the channels and I landed on some of that bad soft core gay porn that plays on one of the 500 channels I get…and I stopped…

FRANK

I usually do.

JACKSON

And I put an honest effort into…appreciating it.

FRANK

How was the lighting?

JACKSON

Harsh—listen, Frank, I *tried.* Like I tried to get myself off to these two beefy guys with tribal tattoos making out. Nearly got there.

FRANK

Nearly?

JACKSON

Alright, you got me, Frank. I *did* get there. Because, I would do anything for you, Frank.

FRANK

Even masturbate to gay soft core, apparently.

JACKSON

(Sadly.)

Anything, Frank.

FRANK

Were they greased up? They're always so greasy…

(Jackson chuckles, but it fades into a small choked up sound as he looks down to his wringing hands. Frank softens at this and moves slightly closer to Jackson.)

What makes people think we want every man wet?

(Jackson smiles, still nervously fiddling with bits of blanket in his hand.)

Jack—

JACKSON

I know I'm hard to love and I've tried every day to change it…but I built my walls up high, Frank. So high, I've become a fucking clown. No one sees the Jackson that tries to just get over his own heterosexuality. No one sees the one that cries looking at ripped up pictures of Monica and him in middle school. No sees me cleaning the cum off my couch after I spent 45 minutes trying to jerk it to greasy men making out—

FRANK

Jesus, Jackson…

JACKSON

People see…Well, I don't really know what they see…but I love you, Frank. I'm sorry I can't love you right, but I love you with as much of me as I understand. With everything I've got to offer. I'm so sorry for trying to make that something base. I just want to give you everything you want, and I thought…that was me—and I would do anything—this doesn't really matter, now, but when I got lunch with Monica and Scott…she…this was sent to my old address…I thought between this and learning to fuck you I had figured it all out…but—

(Jackson grabs a stack of mail from the bedside table and hands it to Frank.)

Here.

FRANK

You're pre-approved, Jack.

JACKSON

Next one.

FRANK

From the—?

JACKSON

M.O.M.A.

FRANK

Who did you fuck at the Museum of Modern Art?

(Jackson smiles.)

JACKSON

Who did you? Seriously, open it. I…already did.

FRANK

(Reading, going from confused, to pained, then to smiling.)

Jackson…

JACKSON

I…curated your wing, Frank. You have *pieces* in a museum, Frank. A big one.

FRANK

I just have the one—

JACKSON

You actually have a wing, now. For like 6 months. But still. *Pieces.* More than one.

(He flips a page of the letter for Frank.)

There's a list. I need you to bring these from your studio…tomorrow actually.

FRANK

What were you going to do if I didn't show up here?

JACKSON

I…just kind of knew you would. When you were ready.

FRANK

Pieces?

JACKSON

Nine.

FRANK

You…just had to be right?

JACKSON

I did. I've always thought your shit should be in a museum and I was utterly offended that you only had the one piece in the one museum so I—

FRANK

So, you've rented me a wing in M.O.M.A.

JACKSON

I called in some favors.

FRANK

Who?

JACKSON

He's banging the love of my life, he owes me…

FRANK

Oh, Jackson…

JACKSON

I'm fine.

FRANK

Why?

JACKSON

Because I love you. So much so, I'm jerking it to dudes, now. I've picked favorites.

FRANK

The one that sort of looks like you?

JACKSON

I'm not that egotistical.

FRANK

Yes, you are.

JACKSON

I am. And, I love you.

(Frank tears up, and pulls Jackson in for a hug. When they break they make an awkward and long eye-contact, then, Frank leans to kiss Jackson, this time; Jackson catches him by the face and pushes back.)

What I did back there was wrong. Because the love I have for you is so much more important. You're Frank and you're my friend. You finger-banged the captain of the softball team in your basement. You could fix my car, if I ever bought one. You've out-painted me every single day of this journey. You made me question my own dick and trust, he and I have never had issues. You love me, and you totally hate that.

We belong to each other. And I'm afraid we belong to each other, forever. Because I got chili in my beard that once…and because you love me—I love you, Frank. I just can't…Frank our love is more special. Fuck fucking, Frank.

FRANK

You lost me at the end there.

JACKSON

(Sadly smiling.)

Okay?

FRANK

O.K.

JACKSON

O.K.?

FRANK

Yeah, O.K.—I'll see you tomorrow, Jack. Thank you.

JACKSON

You're God damned right you'll see me tomorrow; you're doing all the heavy lifting. We've got to hang your master works tomorrow—

FRANK

Tomorrow at one, these nine pieces. I read the thing. Thank you, Jackson. Really.

JACKSON

You're welcome, Frank.

(Frank exits, closing Jackson's bedroom door behind him as the lights fade on the area.)

FRANK

Goodbye, Jack.

JACKSON

Goodnight, Frank.

(Lights up in an art gallery. A few pieces hang on the wall, covered by a sheet or two and a few paintings remain hidden in boxes. Jackson and Monica stand, Monica pacing about while Jackson is very still. A man sits on a bench, reading a newspaper. His face is hidden.)

JACKSON

Late.

MONICA

You're one to talk.

JACKSON

Late isn't like Frank. It's my thing.

SCOTT

(Revealing himself as the newspaper reader.)

Clearly, you've never dated him.

JACKSON

Thank you for coming.

SCOTT

Wouldn't miss it.

(Monica pats Jackson's shoulder.)

MONICA

Jackson…you're—you did good.

JACKSON

I had to do good. There wasn't another choice.

MONICA

(Checking her watch.)

256

Dammit, Frank.

JACKSON

He'll be here.

(Monica regards Jackson.)

What?

MONICA

Nothing…you just—you became someone else for a minute…

JACKSON

What does that mean?

SCOTT

Call him?

(Jackson removes his cell phone from his pocket, Monica smiles.)

JACKSON

What?

MONICA

Nothing.

(He re-pockets his phone.)

JACKSON

Let's just get started. He'll be here.

(Jackson goes to a box and kneels to open it, while Scott and Monica watch, seeming uncomfortable. Jackson seems insistent on ignoring this. Jackson opens the box and looks like he's gasped but is incapable to create sound.)

MONICA

What?

SCOTT

He hates all of them.

JACKSON

No, no, no, no….these are the ones I told him to—

(He stands and begins to back up.)

SCOTT

Jackson?

JACKSON

He's not coming—he—he…these aren't the paintings…

MONICA

Jackson, calm down…

JACKSON

He's not coming! He's—he—

(Jackson runs from the room, full force, Scott stands and goes to the box and lifts a painting he gasps.)

SCOTT

Oh, Frank…

MONICA

What is it?

(Scott turns the painting around to Monica revealing an inspired, colorful portrait of Jackson.)

Oh no…

SCOTT

They're *all*—

(Monica gasps and the lights fade on the area as the pair embraces. The following is heard in blackout.)

FRANK

I live in staggering fear that one day I will have gone so long without seeing you, that I will not be able to paint your visage from memory and that will be the day I will end it, Jack.

JACKSON

We both know you're resolved to painting bowls of fruit and sad still-lives. Portraits are beyond you.

FRANK

Welcome home.

(Again, the sound of sirens wiring is heard. The sounds of the sirens fade into the sound of Jackson's somewhat tearful sounding breath. The lights snap on, sudden, to reveal Jackson, who takes a deep breath; the light tightens to one spot lit area, Jackson steps into. And waits. A second spot lit area appears, but remains empty. Jackson looks over for a moment before coming back to the audience to address them.)

JACKSON

Art.

(Blackout.)

END OF PLAY

About Casey Ross

Ross began writing for the stage her junior year at Hanover College in 2007. Later that year,, through a grant from the college she premiered *Gallery* at the IndyFringe Festival. Since the success of Gallery, Ross has gone on to participate in 8 festivals, including her most recent entry and final part to this series, *Canvas*. Ross's writing career has begun to steadily solidify her as a credible local writer within the Indianapolis theatre scene.

In 2008, Ross's short play *Here's To…* was selected as part of Louisville performance group, Specific Gravity's Elevator Plays 2. Later in 2008, post Ross's graduation, Hanover College selected her full-length play, *Slaying the Dragon* to premiere on the college's main-stage. Post graduation, Ross began writing for the theatre under several commission projects, while still remaining a force at the IndyFringe. Ross was the primary writer for the children's theatre workshops hosted at the Shawnee Summer Theatre for 3 years and helped to grow the program nearly double its size with fresh new plays.

Casey then, spent time touring and directing with the Missoula Children's Theatre for the next two years, before returning to her hometown of Indianapolis and, later, starting her company,   Catalyst Repertory. In was in 2014, when Ross's self proclaimed 'home-base' for theatre, the IndyFringe, celebrated its 10th Anniversary, leading Ross to reprise her successful first work, *Gallery*, with a sequel play, *Portraits*. *Portraits* introduced Ross to partner and co-founder, Taylor Cox, and Catalyst was born. With the welcome official addition of 2013 *The Solidarity* actor, Davey Pelsue, as co-Artistic Director and 3rd Catalyst partner, Catalyst quickly established non-profit status and is now a mainstay Fountain Square and Indianapolis theatre institution. Their 2016 *Equus* was honored as the 2016 Nuvo Best Play of Indy, and their 2017 season opener, Tooth of Crime, has been praised as one of the most exciting stage plays the Indy area has seen. Catalyst Repertory is now in production with its 3rd theatre season and plans to continue bringing their bold new works and adaptations to the city.

About The Geeky Press

The Geeky Press is as much a philosophy as it is an entity.

Brad King launched this little group on April 3, 2014 in hopes of building a vibrant writing community in greater downtown Indianapolis. What he didn't have was much of a plan to make that happen. He launched the website, planned a reading series called The Downtown Writers Jam, and hoped that people would come.

And show up they did. Before long, The Geeky Press grew to include more than 100 writers who participated in writing meetups, retreats, reading series, and other literary gatherings.

Before long, The Geeky Press added three amazing partners: Amber Peckham, who is the wittiest writer of the bunch and who corrals our reading series; Nicole Mathew, who has turned our weekly #WritersHack events into a welcoming writing community; and Elise Lockwood, who helps recruit writers to the podcast and runs the Scripted reading series.

While The Geeky Press is generally run by the three of us, we've encouraged participants to create their own writing spaces. Now we have members like Reid Delehanty, who has started hosting his own #WritersHack.

In other words, this labor of love has become everything we'd hoped it would be.

About Brad

Brad earned his Masters of Journalism from the University of California's Graduate School of Journalism in 2000. Worked for *Wired* and *MIT's Technology Review* as a reporter, multimedia editor, senior editor, and producer. Co-authored *Dungeons & Dreamers: A story of how computer games created a global culture*. And serves as a program board member with South by Southwest Interactive.

On July 1, 2017 he starts his new position as the Editor and Director of Carnegie Mellon University's ETC Press, where he's worked in various capacities since 20067. Before that, he was the co-founder and co-director of Ball State University's Center for Emerging Media Design & Development and a associate professor of journalism.

About Amber

The Geeky Press partner Amber Peckham is an amazing talent. She earned her B.A. in Creative Writing from DePauw University in 2009 and her M.F.A. in Creative Nonfiction at Northwestern University in 2014. She's already developing a reading series along with an essay podcast. Plus, she'll join and help host the #WritersHack. She is just generally be amazing, we're excited to have her on board.

About Nicole

Nicole graduated with a B.A. in English (Writing & Literacy) from IUPUI in 2010. She went back to IUPUI to earn her Masters to teach English, but life took another turn and she wound up becoming a Content Specialist (then later a Project Manager) at eGov Strategies, a small company located in Indianapolis. Between graduation and now, Nicole has been a freelance writer in her spare time, doing a lot of writing for the web. She helps host/organize the #WritersHack and looks forward to connecting with other writers in the Indianapolis area.

About Elise

Elise Lockwood graduated from DePauw University in December 2013 with a B.A. in English Writing. She was awarded the Chad Kostel Memorial Award in Writing and the Barbara Petty Award in Theatre, both from DePauw. Her play *Snatch and Release* will be published in Smith and Krauss, Inc.'s Best Ten-Minute Plays of 2016, coming to shelves this December. In January 2017, her full-length play *Spineless*, will premiere at Bowling Green State University. In real life, Elise is a second-year graduate student in Ball State University's Emerging Media Design and Development master's program.

Other Books by The Geeky Press

HoosierLit: A Literary Magazine by The Geeky Press, Spring 2017

HoosierLit: A Literary Magazine by The Geeky Press is a publication that features some of the best fiction, non-fiction, essays, poetry, and script writing by Indiana writers.

http://www.thegeekypress.com/hoosierlit

Bad Jobs & Bullshit: It's Unlikely That We Will Be Missed (Vol. 1)

We're just people who have worked a lot of bad jobs, and put up with a lot of bullshit, and decided we wanted to hear about how that same phenomenon happened to others. We think you'll find the mix of essays, short stories, and poems in this collection speak to common experiences and make you feel less alone in your struggle against the grinding machine of entropy.

http://www.thegeekypress.com/badjobs

www.ingramcontent.com/pod-product-compliance
Lightning Source LLC
Chambersburg PA
CBHW080906170526
45158CB00008B/2009